The

BOOKS

that

CHANGED

MY LIFE

———•———

REFLECTIONS BY 100 AUTHORS,
ACTORS, MUSICIANS, AND
OTHER REMARKABLE PEOPLE

——— Edited by ———

BETHANNE PATRICK

Regan Arts.
NEW YORK

Regan Arts.

Introduction and compilation copyright
© 2016, 2020 by Bethanne Patrick.

Individual essays copyright © 2016, 2020 by their authors

All rights reserved, including the right to reproduce this book or portions thereof in any form whatsoever. For information, email pr@reganarts.com.

Originally published in hardcover by Regan Arts in 2016.

First Regan Arts paperback edition, 2020

Library of Congress Control Number: 2015946442

ISBN 978-1-68245-156-4

Interior design by Nancy Singer
Cover design by Chin-Yee Lai
Cover photograph by Tamara Staples/Getty Images

10 9 8 7 6 5 4 3 2 1

To my mother, Julia, who nurtured my love
of books and reading—and whose performances of stories, from
Babar the King to "The Cask of Amontillado," showed me the
many ways in which written words can be brought to life.

CONTENTS

INTRODUCTION

BY BETHANNE PATRICK

Over the last fifteen years of my work as a writer, critic, and author, I've included the words "and above all, a reader" in many professional biographies. Although it's long defunct and is probably being used by someone else, my very first attempt at a blog was called *The Reading Writer*.

Forget about the chicken and the egg; for me, the paramount conundrum has always been "Which came first, reading or writing?" Neither question is easy, or even possible, to answer. You could argue at length (and somewhere a group of academics is already doing so) about what constitutes "reading" versus "writing." If an infant's first sight is her mother's face, does that mean reading wins? Or was that baby writing out thoughts in her neonatal brain during gestation? This is what happens when you spend too much time considering literature in an academic setting. *Caveat lector.*

A much simpler idea is that most of us start out as listeners. Our society may not rely on oral tradition much these days, but families definitely do. No matter what happens to books and publishing, we know about the great good that comes from parents reading to and with their children. Hearing stories told helps young brains to form and grow. A parent's attention combined with reading aloud strengthens bonds of love and compassion and community. A house that holds books on its shelves and reading in high esteem is a house more likely to raise curious, bright, contented, and responsible individuals.

However—and this bears out anecdotally, because I heard it from several dozen of the people you'll meet in these pages— nothing seems to compare to the thrill of beginning to read on one's own. So many writers, in particular, remember the first book they held and decoded without adult assistance. Reading has been described as everything from a frigate (Emily Dickinson) to a rainbow (LeVar Burton), the common idea being one of magical transport. Say what you will about music, film, television, dance, painting, theater, sculpture—only text on a page can be sustained at such length that a person can both get lost in it and create his or her own version of it simultaneously. Reading has power. It can be education or entertainment, solace or spark, one time only or many times over.

Books change people's lives, before they can even turn a page and long after they've mastered what that page holds. Some of the men and women I interviewed for this book had trouble narrowing down their book choices, but no one had trouble thinking of at least one. These people include professional writers, but others are musicians, CEOs, politicians, actors, comedians, activists, cartoonists, military service members, journalists, and chefs. Some loved to read from early childhood; others disliked reading; and still others were dyslexic or came from households where books were scarce. Some of the individuals included have PhDs, JDs, MDs, and medals; others spent time on the streets, in prison, or laid up from illness. They are men, women, gay, lesbian, straight, married, single, parents, child-free, young, old, city dwellers, country strong, Jewish, Christian, Muslim, Buddhist, agnostic, atheist, liberal, conservative, natives, immigrants, famous, little-known, and everything in between. Some are people I've interviewed multiple times, and others were strangers to me until we spoke. Some are friends for life, and one, who was an admired colleague, died just a few weeks before this project was completed.

All of them understood, when I approached them for interviews, that the question of which book changed your life is a serious one; they also understood that choosing to use part of this compilation's proceeds to benefit 826 National is a serious good. Encouraging young people to write, making sure that they have a safe place to write, and giving them time to create both individually and in community—these are seriously important benefits of 826 centers in cities from New York to LA to Chicago to Boston. The people in this book, readers all, want young writers to know how important reading can be to anyone's life, and they also want to allow young writers to hope that one day their efforts may change someone's life.

One of the parts of this project that makes me happiest is that although no one interviewed was given a list from which to choose and although none of them were told others' choices in advance, there is only one duplicate title on the list. That doesn't mean all of the books spoken about meet any parameters. There are children's books, poetry collections, biographies, classic novels, modern favorites, and even a comic book included. What this says to me, and I hope to you, is that life-changing books don't come with "Read Here" labels attached. They have as much to do with the reader's perspective as with the author's voice.

Which is why I will tell you the book that changed my life

is one that I haven't mentioned before in a blog post, book list, or essay. When I was about twenty-five, I was wavering about what came next (like most twentysomethings do). My husband was planning to attend law school, and it seemed sensible for me to do the same, given my social-science-dense college transcript.

My book group at the time was a serious and diligent one, but most of its members were also serious Lutherans who belonged to the same church, and some of their selections were heavily theological. I didn't mind, as those books at least made me feel I was using my brain after long days corralling high school students as a history teacher.

But in the late winter of 1988, someone in the group selected a novel by a Japanese author I'd never heard of: *Silence* by Shusaku Endo. First published in 1966, a winner of the Tanizaki Prize, and considered by many to be one of the best novels of the twentieth century, *Silence* is the story of a Portuguese missionary to seventeenth-century Japan whose fidelity to Roman Catholic dogma is challenged by armed persecutors of local Christians in hiding.

No, *Silence* did not effect my conversion. However, I was then, and remain, a seriously spiritual person, and I'd never before encountered a book that was both a testament to faith and a work of art. It doesn't matter, when you read Endo, whether you are a devout Christian or a committed atheist. Although his material is more overtly religious than, say, a fellow Catholic like Flannery O'Connor's, like O'Connor, Endo uses his beliefs to explore the moral center that unites the greatest works of literature in all world cultures. His fiction wastes no time on proselytizing. It focuses on character, conflict, and truth.

I knew as I took in the hard, sad, and often terrifying events in *Silence* that I did not want to spend my time discussing contracts and torts. Endo may not have tried to evangelize, but I wanted to. I wanted to tell everyone I knew about this book. And I learned quickly what most evangelists do: not everyone wants to hear about the book that changed your life.

However, a friend from college to whom I rhapsodized about Endo's novel told me that even though she wasn't interested in reading it, she could tell that it had truly moved me. "You love to talk about books and their authors, Bethanne," she said. "You love to do that, and you are good at it. You shouldn't go to law school. You should study literature."

To say that I was flabbergasted is an understatement. I'd been such a flop in my undergraduate English classes that I switched majors to political science. No one had ever encouraged me to study literature; that was for my smart classmates, the ones who decorated their walls and wastepaper baskets with rejection slips from *The New Yorker* and *The Atlantic*.

The rest of the story can be mercifully shortened, but really, who makes a decision about graduate school based on one comment from her friend Sue? Small wonder I didn't pursue a doctorate in English. However, I did finish my MA, and the semesters I spent reading, analyzing, and discussing great prose and poetry with great minds (I mean my professors, not you theory-heads, just to be clear) are among the most electrifying months of my life.

Shusaku Endo's *Silence* actually helped me course-correct. Even though I didn't stay on the path I'd expected to when I set out, I knew that I would find a way to make my life and career involve deep, sustained reading and writing. A book changed my life. A book might change your life. Won't you join me in hearing how it changed the lives of one hundred other readers?

DIANA ABU-JABER

on *"The Tell-Tale Heart"*
by Edgar Allan Poe

"I wanted to get on that stage, too"

It's such a latticework effect, you know? Even though my mom was a reading teacher, I wasn't really raised in a household of books. It's funny, I never really thought about that before, but it's true. My parents read big thick mass-market paperback thrillers, probably because they both worked hard and just wanted to relax when they picked up a book.

But my mother did bring home lots of fairy tales, which became very important to me, collections of the Brothers Grimm, creation tales, folktales from around the world. Some of them were pretty dark, and I loved that. It set that stage for Poe.

I went through a long adolescent period of being gripped by Edgar Allan Poe, really enamored with his work. I was captivated by the story, the voice, and the tension of "The Tell-Tale Heart." The sense you get of a rational madman!

"The Tell-Tale Heart" in particular was so subtle and so

sensitive, because the narrator keeps attempting to reassure the reader that he's not mad—but he keeps giving himself away through his actions. And so for a young reader like myself, it was riveting to see how that worked—a character who gives himself away, creates a kind of shadow, if you will. There is a sense of dimension there, the feeling that you can walk around the character and you can look not only at his face, but also at the back of his head.

These kinds of characters reveal more than they realize they're revealing, through their speech and actions. And it's such a beautiful, subtle technique, so effective in the context of something like the gruesome murder that takes place in "The Tell-Tale Heart." There's something fascinating about seeing a delicate technique used to depict such a dramatic event.

It's something I talk with my students about a lot—the idea of three-dimensional writing, when readers know more about the characters than they know about themselves. I feel like that's when writing is really the most electric.

And it's difficult to teach, but you can kind of describe it and point to examples of literature and let people kind of think about that. Usually people really get it. Everyone knows someone who got involved with the wrong person. We can see it when it happens to someone else, but the person involved never can, because they're too close to it.

I was introduced to Poe in high school, by a wonderful English teacher who read a number of the stories out loud. Having someone give voice to these narrators made them enthralling; it was an extra kick that made me start paying attention. I was really paying attention to voice, and I guess I was really captivated because I was raised in such a loud household that I couldn't hear myself.

All of my Jordanian relatives on my dad's side were great storytellers, and they were mostly big, loud men. I would be at the dinner table, and I got to be the audience, but I always wanted to be a storyteller. I wanted to get on that stage, too.

It became very important to me to hear my own voice. Poe not only had a singular voice, he was so subversive, so wicked, so naughty—all the things I wasn't raised to or allowed to be. And so I saw these things as one piece. Speaking, having a strong voice, having a subversive sensibility, having darkness, and allowing darkness to come through all came together for me at that time. I started writing my own early pieces back then, and I think that's how I knew that Poe was having this impact on me.

Diana Abu-Jaber is most recently the author of Birds of Paradise *as well as the award-winning memoir* The Language of Baklava *and the bestselling novels* Origin *and* Crescent.

HEATHER B. ARMSTRONG

on *The Warmth of Other Suns* by Isabel Wilkerson

"It's time that we recognize our privilege"

I knew immediately which book I wanted to share. It's *The Warmth of Other Suns: The Epic Story of America's Great Migration* by Isabel Wilkerson. I learned about it earlier this year during a conference at which a dear friend of mine called all of us in the room out for caring about feminism and other things but not speaking up about racism.

I went right up to her afterward and said, "Kelly, you made me sit back in my chair, because I know you were talking to all of us, but you were speaking directly to me. I am so sorry. What can I do, as a white woman, to change this problem?"

She didn't castigate me, she just told me about this book and said, "Start here. Start with this." She showed me so much mercy. She wasn't angry with me. She wasn't being pedantic. She shared something that would give me the language to talk about the problem of racism in our country.

What's really important to me, in this sweeping, beautifully written book, is that it's about three African-American people who sought "the warmth of other suns"—that's a phrase from the poet Richard Wright—in the North and West of the United States during decades of the twentieth century in which it was simply impossible for people of color to live with any dignity in the South. Whether or not they can do so today is not something for me to argue, and that's part of what I learned in reading Wilkerson's book.

I'm from the South, from Tennessee. My parents grew up in the Jim Crow South. I grew up, in Memphis, in a South where racial relations are still so tense. I grew up with opinions I should not have had, because I was taught those things, my parents were taught those things.

But I got out! Here I am in Utah. I'm not a racist! I'm not doing anything racist. Right?

The trouble was, I wasn't doing anything. I wasn't speaking up against racism. I wasn't asking questions about how to heal racism. It totally changed my life, this book. It changed my behavior. It changed who I want to be and what I do. It's time that we recognize our privilege, we white people, and we recognize our responsibility to dismantle it. Black people are tired. Until we, the white people, take steps to change things, it's never going to be any different.

We don't have to suffer what our fellow citizens have had to suffer. I've been teaching my children not to think about color, not to see color. You know what? People of color are sick of *that* shit. No no no no no no no. Don't teach your children to be color-blind. We have a problem, and that is not going to solve it.

I will never have to worry about one of my daughters being pulled over at a routine traffic stop and being injured. I will never have to worry about her going into a store and having someone gasp because she's entered it. People of color have to deal with situations like those and worse all the time.

Wilkerson's book is on my e-reader, and I've highlighted page after page and I go back to reread those passages all the time. I want to share it with Marlo, my eldest, when she gets to middle school, and in the meantime, share it with as many friends, relatives, and strangers who read my blog and my books and listen to what I say as possible. What could be more important in forming an online community than using it to solve real-life problems?

Heather B. Armstrong is a speaker, writer, and pioneer in the world of online writing and advertising. Her website, dooce, was one of the first personal websites to sign with Federated Media Publishing in 2005. Armstrong has written a New York Times *bestseller,* It Sucked and Then I Cried: How I Had a Baby, a Breakdown, and a Much Needed Margarita.

MARGARET ATWOOD

on "Grimm's Fairy Tales"
by the Brothers Grimm

"It was good stuff"

I had a reading mother. It's the best thing. She did all the voices, and at one point we were living in Sault Ste. Marie and she would read to us each evening. She attracted an audience of all the neighborhood children. We would all sit on the floor and listen to her.

She was basically broadcasting without radio or TV, to a rapt group of listeners. She would start with Beatrix Potter, a mistress of style and indirection, and very succinct. And then she continued with various children's classics of the time, such as *Wind in the Willows, Peter Pan, Alice's Adventures in Wonderland*, and other favorites.

The first book that I can remember reading for myself, in addition to the funny papers, to which I was addicted, was the collected Grimm's fairy tales, in an edition that came out in the mid-1940s. It was an Athenaeum book; a very good translation. My parents sent away for it by mail order, not knowing quite what was in it. This was before the 1950s editions, which were heavy on princesses and downplayed all the violence.

In our edition, the stories were more horrifying. All the original red-hot shoes and gouged-out eyeballs were left in. It was good stuff. My younger sister didn't like those stories; they were too much for her. She only liked "The Twelve Dancing Princesses." She was a more nervous child than we were.

Did they "change my life?" Who knows what it would have been like otherwise? But these stories did give me a large repertoire of story types. The next things that we got were children's versions of Greek myths, which were joined by Native American mythology. And because we were in Canada, where church and state were not separated at that time, we also got a lot of scripture in school. Every day! Some of it was incomprehensible to me at that age, but I can recognize most Bible quotations. That's very useful if you then go on to study Western literature, because these stories are part of our literary foundation: Greek myth, the Bible, European folklore, and, now, Native North American stories. All of these are in my work, in one way or another.

So is biology: because my father was a biologist, the books I read included biology textbooks, so I was reading about tadpoles and what's inside a worm. This kind of material has also become part of my work, more recently. I didn't have to start from scratch when I was writing *Oryx and Crake:* I already had address to that way of understanding the world.

Do I read anything life-changing now? I'm. Too. Old. You have to go back to a person's youth to unearth the books that changed them. When did I begin to write with the conscious idea that I would be a writer? When I was sixteen. I started with a bad poem, then another bad poem. That went on for a while. I thought they were wonderful at the time, of course.

In high school we had a curriculum full of classics. We read Thomas Hardy—*The Mayor of Casterbridge*, *Tess of the d'Urbervilles*, that sort of thing. We read a lot of Shakespeare, and the Romantic and Victorian poets. If you want to know more about what the teaching style was like, then go to my book *Moral Disorder* and read the chapter called "My Last Duchess." We didn't learn anything about authors, but we studied the texts themselves in great detail, and we paid a lot of attention to style. In retrospect, that wasn't a bad kind of education for someone who wanted to be a writer.

The English teacher in the story was real, and her name really was Miss Bessie. I showed her one of my bad poems, and she said, "Dear, this must be very good, because I can't understand it all."

Margaret Atwood is the author of more than forty volumes of poetry, children's literature, fiction, and nonfiction, but is best known for her novels, which include The Edible Woman *(1969),* The Handmaid's Tale *(1985),* The Robber Bride *(1994),* Alias Grace *(1996), and* The Blind Assassin, *which won the prestigious Booker Prize in 2000. Her latest,* The Heart Goes Last, *was released in 2015.*

GINA BARRECA

on *Remember Me*
by Fay Weldon

"I never looked up, not once"

When I was a graduate student at Cambridge University and miserable, which is par for the course—wait, it was the weekend I would have graduated from college, but I graduated early, so I was just about to go to Cambridge. But I was already miserable, because my boyfriend at the time wouldn't come with me to Paris, where I had never been. I had never been anywhere out of the country except for England, and I wanted to go to Paris, but I had to do it on the cheap.

And so a friend of mine from Long Island, a high school friend who was working at a psychiatric fellowship or institution, happened to be working there and came with me. We were going to take the train to the hovercraft, which doesn't even exist anymore, I think. So this was the mid-to-late 1970s, and even though I'm on my first trip to Paris and with my best friend in the world, I'm miserable because of the boyfriend. I was afraid that he was going to forget me during this four-day trip.

At the train station, I went to a book stall. I had just finished all my academic work, so to pick up a novel to read for pleasure and escape was a treat. I chose one called *Remember Me*. I'd never heard of the author, but it was one of those mass-market paperbacks with dyed edges, which tended then to signal a juicy, easy read. "Perfect," I thought.

First of all, it turned out to be a ghost story, and it was amazing, the story of a teenage girl's relationship with her dead mother. But it was also hilarious. I had never read anything like it in terms of the use of language, the syntax, the blend of vernacular and sophisticated language, along with vivid characters and an astonishing pace. And I had already done a lot of reading! I was a ferocious reader, and I'd read a lot of funny women writers—Jean Kerr, Shirley Jackson. But I'd never read anything this funny, literary, and sophisticated all at once.

Here I am, on the train in France, and I never looked up, not once. My friend was elbowing me, saying, "Look! French cows!" and I was saying, "Wait, let me read this to you!"

I immediately wanted to read everything that the author, Fay Weldon, had ever written. I did, and I loved her books, her writing, her voice, and her themes so much that I chose to write my dissertation about Weldon. I sent her a letter through the BBC because she'd just done a story for them, never thinking I would get a response.

My note was simple, on one of those aerogram foldable thingamajigs. "Dear Ms. Weldon, I just want to let you know that in part my PhD dissertation will be on your works. This is not to say I'm going to dig up your garden looking for old manuscripts, but I just wanted to make you aware of it. Thank you very much, Gina Barreca."

Two and a half weeks later I get an envelope containing a

letter that says, and I quote: "Dear Gina Barreca, By all means dig up the garden. You can keep the manuscripts. You can have the manuscripts. We shall plant bulbs. Yours, Fay Weldon."

I fell in love. It was my first girl crush, and I swooned. By then, I was a graduate teaching assistant, and I brought Fay over for her first US reading. Her publisher and agent hadn't thought she had a real readership here, but I filled the house. It was an audience of something like four hundred people. They'd been waiting. Her publisher and agent saw this, and sort of changed their minds toward her American situation. Her next book, *The Hearts and Lives of Men*, got the front page of the *New York Times Book Review*, a write-up by John Updike. She sent me a telegram saying, "All your doing."

She changed my life; I may or may not have changed hers. But she gave me away at my second wedding. And she taught me that as a writer, you can respond to everyone. Sometimes there's nothing you can do to help someone, but if there isn't, you can at least give them advice or encouragement. Fay Weldon answered my letter, and it changed everything for me.

Gina Barreca teaches feminist theory at the University of Connecticut and writes a weekly column nationally syndicated by Tribune News Service, and her next book is If You Lean In, Will Men Just Look Down Your Blouse? Questions and Thoughts for Loud, Smart Women in Turbulent Times.

LOUIS BAYARD

on *David Copperfield*
by Charles Dickens

"A common man on the page"

When I was about twelve, I had a copy of *David Copperfield* by Charles Dickens, bound in red morocco leather, with one of those ribbons—what are they called?—that holds your place. I cherished the ribbon as much as I did the book, would wrap it around my finger while I read, place it reverently between the pages when I was finished. It wasn't the same as a regular bookmark. It seemed integral to the book itself, and it fascinated me. It was this elegant way of marking the beginning and end of reading; there was something almost liturgical about it.

The edges of the paper were saffron, I remember. It must have been a gift, and I've since lost track of who gave it to me and where it is, but it was completely mine (although I did have a way of appropriating books that were not mine). I read the novel two or three times over the course of my adolescence. I don't often reread books now, but *David Copperfield* is one that I'm sure I'll pick up again—and now that we've talked, maybe sooner rather than later.

When I think about the first line, when Dickens talks about being the hero of your own life—that's something I'm still striving for. That, to me, is about as inspiring a concept as you can have. Back then, I think I had very traditional notions of heroism and bravery, and courage—very masculine. Now it's about becoming the owner of your own life, not letting other people live it for you.

While this didn't point me toward, say, the military, it did make me want to be a writer. I read the book in a kind of trance, just wanting more and more with each page. At a certain point, I felt as if there were no beginning and no end. When I did finish, it seemed to me that Dickens was the most powerful person I could imagine. The power to make a person—the reader—a kind of slave, I was just in awe of that. Among other things, Dickens is such a wonderful entertainer. There's always something, a detail that delights you or keeps you engaged. I was so captivated by his career that I had this whole parallel career worked out in which I wrote my first book at the same age that he had written his first book. Well, that didn't work out, but when I wrote *Mr. Timothy*, it was homage with true passion and fealty behind it.

I've always wanted to move and entertain people in the way that Dickens did. He's still the greatest influence on my own work. I love his values, his political values, his passionate fights against injustice, but I also love his attention to entertaining the reader. The serial form was something he believed in, that you had to meet the reader halfway. He wasn't interested in a mandarin aesthetic of art. He was very much a common man on the page. There was something really important in the way I fell for every trick he put in front of me. Even if I could see that it was a trick, could see that a character was placed there to make me feel pity or scorn, I loved it. I loved every bit of it. He understood the human love for cliffhangers, and I think he anticipated something very popular today, these TV series like *The Sopranos* and *Breaking Bad* that we follow even when they lead us into very strange places.

Something that was quite important for me when I was younger, before I was given this beautiful edition of *David Copperfield*, was the Classics Illustrated comic book series. You could read them again and again and again, but they didn't spoil you for the full version of a book. It was a wonderful preparation for reading. I recently found one based on *The Invisible Man*, and I was fascinated to see how faithful it was to the original novel. I should get on eBay and see if I can find the *David Copperfield* edition. It sounds silly, in retrospect, but I believe that there are many ways to become hooked on stories, and if a cartoon can lead you to Dickens? Nothing wrong with that.

Louis Bayard writes historical thrillers, including Roosevelt's Beast, The School of Night, The Black Tower, The Pale Blue Eye, *and* Mr. Timothy. *A* New York Times *Notable Author, he has been nominated for both the Edgar and Dagger awards and named one of* People *magazine's top authors of the year.*

MAYIM BIALIK

on *Hopscotch*
by Julio Cortázar

"A form of communication"

I come from a family of readers. My parents are both English teachers. I inherited my father's library, an amazing legacy, and I am currently designing a library/bedroom around those fifty boxes of books.

It's an amazing legacy, but a sad one, too: my father died four months ago, from cancer.

In the last month of his life, when he was in hospice, I started reading to him. We didn't get very far, but it was an amazing experience, very, very emotionally dense and very beautiful. My mother would drift in and out as I read to my dad, and it became something that gave shape to very difficult days.

The book I read to my father was *Hopscotch* by Julio Cortázar. The novel was a huge influence on my dad. He even wrote a letter to Cortázar in 1965—and got a response. That letter is still inside my father's 1966 copy of the book that he took from the library.

Reading to my dad was a way to give him a sense of calm. Words and music were so important to him, so I tried to give that to him. At first we would sing together, but it became harder and harder for him to participate. I knew reading out loud would be soothing. He would request it, and sometimes I knew it was too heavy, but it really served as kind of a placeholder—and even when he couldn't actively communicate, it was a form of communication, because I was reading to him what he had passed to me.

After he died, my mother dropped *Hopscotch* in our local library's book drop, not realizing it was my dad's purloined copy. I went and asked for its return, and I'm glad I did. Besides the author's letter, in the pocket where the library card goes my father had a stack of about a dozen index cards, the kind he made notes on constantly. One of the cards just has the word "enmeshed." He's been gone for four months and it feels like both an eternity and an instant.

My dad was the firstborn American in his family, and he rebelled against his traditional immigrant background by loving really, really esoteric stuff, like Cortázar. He was his family's liberal, their broad thinker, and for my parents' generation the possibility of this new world led naturally to becoming a teacher if you weren't going to be a doctor or a lawyer. My father loved words, this language that his parents didn't even really speak very well. He was really an artist, a bohemian poet, but although he never thought of himself as someone following a poet's career, he maintained his awe of literature, and reading for reading's sake, his entire life.

Even when I was a teen and spending most of my time reading scripts, that was no excuse to fall behind in my reading. My father would make reading lists for me, lists that I would become determined to conquer, and that became a huge part of our life together, something that linked us; books told the story of our family, in a way.

I still read a lot, although given my profession as a scientist and my busy life as a parent I read a lot more nonfiction now—including books on meditation. I'm reading one by Sharon Salzberg right now. I try to keep up with *The New Yorker* and *Harper's*, magazines that my father loved so much. I do read to my children, but I grew up in a home where Dr. Seuss was considered a little silly, so the books I choose for them tend to be a bit more wordy and narrative driven.

Mayim Bialik has a PhD in neuroscience from UCLA; she also plays a neuroscientist on TV, in The Big Bang Theory. *Bialik, who starred in the 1990s sitcom* Blossom, *lives with her two sons in Los Angeles.*

ROBIN BLACK

on *The Diary of Alice James*

"Maybe there's more to the picture here"

I first read T*he Diary of Alice James* when I was in my late teens. Alice was the younger sister of Henry and William (there were also two other sons in there who weren't in the literary world) and she was very likely as brilliant as her two high-achieving brothers, but, perhaps entirely because of her sex, was never encouraged to do anything with her brains. In fact, she was routinely teased and belittled, by her father and also by William who often spoke to and about her as though she were the object of his romantic affection, accusing her of toying with his heart. If, in some abstract sense, Alice had the potential to achieve what her brothers achieved, she never did so. Institutionalized for emotional distress several times in her youth, she ended up, in adulthood, bedridden with something like a "nervous disposition"—the sort of condition with which women of her time were often diagnosed. And while in bed she kept a diary.

Before I realized the ways in which I identified with Alice James, I fell in love with her voice, brilliant and funny as hell, and not particularly nice. She could paint pictures of those she knew that were both hilarious and devastating. And then came the deeper resonances for me. I too have two older brothers, and, like Alice, I too was the younger sister who could not achieve. While they were were top of their classes, accomplished musicians, attending Ivy League schools, I graduated in the bottom of my class, could never learn to read music, and was rejected by all but one college to which I applied. I suffered from very serious, undiagnosed ADD, as well as some other less serious learning disabilities, anxiety, and depression, all of which contributed to a girlhood of frustration and sadness.

In a sense, Alice's diary felt both like a companion in failure and like a beacon of hope. Yes, she never achieved in any of the classic, recognized ways, but it was so clear that she was smart and a gifted writer, it gave me some sense that I too might have some undetected potential. *Wait a minute, maybe there's more to the picture here. Maybe the little sister actually can be smart too!* Alice was a kind of aspirational figure for me, not because I wanted to land in bed for life, but because I hoped that I too had a kind of secret intelligence that nobody, including me, had yet accessed.

Yet despite all the parallels, it's hard to explain the gut level on which she mattered to me, or the range of emotions she brought out in me, from hope for myself to a kind of glee at the nasty acuity of the social skewerings that pepper her writing. From the bed into which she had collapsed, she energized me. Though there was no immediate change to my course. That state of feeling trapped by my own failings and failures lasted until I was in my forties; but all through those years Alice James helped me maintain a private belief that being a low-achieving "girl" in a high-achieving family didn't necessarily mean that one has nothing to say, that one's potential is, in fact, as limited as one's performance.

I reread Alice's diary every couple of years, and when I go back to it, I get an ever-larger sense of a wide intelligence that does not conform to any gender stereotypes—which may well be why her generation found no use for it. I also have a much deeper sense of the waste that was made of her gifts. When I was younger, I may have been angered by that—but it was on my own behalf. Now, I am angered for her. As was she, clearly, all that anger finding its way into the satire she wrote, and the sharp, cutting edge to all her words. She was constrained by her time and by her family, but she got that message of injustice across, and that is her revenge.

Robin Black's short story collection, If I Loved You, I Would Tell You This, *was a finalist for the Frank O'Connor International Short Story Award and an* O, The Oprah Magazine *summer reading pick. Her debut novel,* Life Drawing, *has received critical acclaim. Black's forthcoming book,* Crash Course: Fifty-Two Essays from Where Writing and Life Collide, *will be out from Engine Books in April 2016.*

AMY BLOOM

on *The Deptford Trilogy*
by Robertson Davies

"Like being on a bicycle again"

I'm a big fan of dark humor, that supple, muscular trope, which is for me as comforting and familiar as nightfall. But it wasn't until I read Robertson Davies in the Middletown Public Library that I saw it put on a page in a way that I could relate to and recognize, at just that moment.

When I discovered him, I was a mother of young children—and young myself—meaning I was considerably overwhelmed. I would bundle the children up and head to the library, which was the only warm place I felt we could all find something worthwhile to do.

I settled my girls with the worn blocks and headless dolls that are particular to public libraries and I found Davies's *The Deptford Trilogy*. I got to read for ten uninterrupted minutes and the pages lifted me out of my intensely enveloping and demanding life. It was like being a kid on a bicycle. The black marks on the page took off the restraining hands and I was off, and flying.

I didn't write anything of my own for five more years. I had a full-time job and three kids. What came early and easily to me was not writing, but parenting. These sprawling, acerbic, compassionate novels by Davies poked me, comforted me, teased me. I was up at midnight, reading this bearded, irascible, demanding old man and I was grateful.

You'd be hard-pressed to find a lot of traces of Robertson Davies in my own work, but nevertheless, there was some tectonic shift after I read these books. I thought, *Oh, yeah. Maybe so, maybe this is something I will do.* It was a kind of permission to write as I intended to write, which was with humor and incident and the unexpected. It was less "Oh, that's what I aspire to" than "Oh, oh, I see that. Let me take another look." It was more of what is possible, a road sign pointing out: "You could take this exit."

Although I'm choosing Davies, due to that particular, needful time in my own life, I have to mention another author: Carol Shields, another Canadian, as it happens. How is it that this woman who won a Pulitzer in 1995, one of the greatest novelists I've ever read, a brilliant storyteller and fearless experimenter in form, is nearly unknown?

Larry's Party. The Stone Diaries. Are you kidding me? Are you *kidding* me? Gorgeous prose. Humor so dark it tints all that you see. Compassion, wit, and vision. These books aren't pompous doorsteps. They don't preen. They don't digress. They are just brilliant, illuminating novels about life. That's all.

Sometimes young women writers ask me: Why are books by a man more known than books by a woman? The answer is because we give birth, and all those writers and readers, whether they're male or female, have mothers. Not everybody has a father, but everybody has a mother. It's just like that Nora Ephron movie years ago where the stand-up comic says, "If your children have a choice between you being happy and successful in LA, successfully pursuing your dream, or weeping suicidally in the room right next door after you make them a grilled cheese sandwich, they'll take the sandwich."

The fact is no one gives a shit if Mom is the president of the United States, as long as Mom is making a grilled cheese sandwich and saying, "Oh, honey, here's a napkin." When women accomplish things besides mothering, I think there's a feeling that some bit of mothering, some piece of what we collectively need has been stolen away. *Why is she doing that? Why isn't she paying attention to me?*

My own feeling about it, I'm sorry to say, is that until men give birth, it's not going to change.

That doesn't mean I'm not rereading Evan S. Connell. Or Dickens. Or Roth. Or Percival Everett. I do, all the time. I have all the crappy paperback versions of their novels that I loved and still love and refer to regularly. And my hardcovers of Davies and Shields are up there on the shelf right next to them.

Amy Bloom's most recent novel is Lucky Us. *She has also written* Away: A Novel *and three collections of short stories, and is Wesleyan University's Distinguished Writer in Residence.*

DEBORAH BLUM

on *The Rubáiyát of Omar Khayyam*

"To create that picture in your mind"

I started my freshman year at Florida State University planning to be a chemist. And I might have been if I hadn't turned out to be such a klutzy dreamer in the lab. In my first year there, I first set my hair on fire and then forced a slightly panicked lab evacuation after accidentally creating a small toxic cloud at my Bunsen burner. I realized that if I really planned to survive into my sophomore year, I was not going to be a chemist.

Meanwhile, I decided to experiment elsewhere by taking a poetry class. It didn't take me long to realize that wasn't going to work either. Too personal, too intimate. I started writing poems, beautiful poems, I thought, but emotionally safe. I literally wrote an epic poem on nothing but what ice looks like to the Inuit, which led my professor to say: "What are you doing? I'm on the seventh page of your latest description of ice crystals."

Not entirely directly, but this eventually brought me to science journalism—a love of chemistry, a love of the music of language. I still believe that no one uses language with more gorgeous precision than poets. I still read poetry, admire it, and it remains hugely influential in the way I think about telling a story. And one of my favorite books is a copy of *The Rubaiyat of Omar Khayyam*, currently sitting on a bookshelf in my mother's house. Her father, my grandfather, gave it to my grandmother in the 1930s. It's battered but it's still a physically beautiful book, glowing with gilt and color. And with poetry that illuminates the natural world.

It's always made me think about the writer I want to be. I hope someday to infuse my own writing with that sense of nature unfolding like poetry, have the ability to capture that fleeting shimmer of light. That book, which I read every time we visited my grandparents' home and which I have yet to pry away from my mother, taught me to see nature as something lyrical.

You might wonder why it was such a treasured copy. My grandfather was a railroad lawyer who just loved literature. The family story was that he'd once dreamed of being an actor; when we arrived at their place, in Louisville, Kentucky, he would always pull a Shakespeare play off the shelf so that we could read it together.

I think he saw the book as both a gift of love and of himself. And so did she. They must have looked at it so often together that it's no wonder that the outer binding along the spine is broken. So when I see it, of course, I see more than an old book of verse. I see family, and love, and a shared affection for the power of words.

And when I'm thinking about how to describe a changing sky, I still I turn to FitzGerald's translation of Khayyam's lines: "Awake! For Morning in the Bowl of Night has flung the Stone and that's the song that puts the Stars to Flight." I just love that image of the sun coming up in that deep bowl of light, the way an image from long ago still resonates today.

And it offers me a lesson as a science writer. Science can often seem abstract to people. But human beings are a very visual species. We can understand things when we see them; when we create a mental image of how something works, it becomes tangible to us. I remember being at a meeting of the American Astronomical Society. Researchers were describing a blast of energy out in deep space that seemed to be pushing young stars forward. And one of my colleagues, a writer at the *Los Angeles Times*, described it as like stars surfing a silver wave. That's not the scientific description, obviously, but it creates a memorable picture in the reader's mind. I still remember it. And that again tells you something about the power of language and image and even poetry.

And talking about this makes me see that imagined wash of stars, that breaking of light in the morning, that amazing poetic sense of the world in which we live. Which means that I don't actually need to have my grandfather's old book at hand. But someday…

Deborah Blum directs the Knight Science Journalism program at the Massachusetts Institute of Technology. Her five books include The Poisoner's Handbook *(2010) and* The Monkey Wars *(1994), which was based on a series that won 1992 Pulitzer for Beat Reporting for* The Sacramento Bee.

GESINE

BULLOCK-PRADO

on *Der Struwwelpeter*
by Heinrich Hoffmann

"I love the absurdity of it"

For everyone, there are things that change your life at different times, but I cannot hesitate in identifying the book that first changed mine, which was a German children's book called *Der Struwwelpeter*, by Heinrich Hoffmann. My mother, Helga, was German, and this book is very, very typically a German children's book, which is to say that it's full of maiming and mayhem. One of the first images from the book is of a small boy with one of his thumbs sliced off and bleeding in the air. It's horrible, horrible imagery of what can happen if you're a bad child. Listen, *Kindern*, if you're bad, the following things can happen to you! It's all meant in fun. German fun.

There's nothing light about it; it's full of heaviness and gore. But it's also incredibly funny and absurd, as well as beautifully executed. The drawings and their coloration are so precise—no drop of blood left behind. You can see the sinew and bone of the thumbsucking boy's hacked-off digits.

So why, how, could this possibly change my life? There are lots of German children's books like this—and there are also lots of German folklore figures like this. Some children have Santa Claus; we had Krampus. In Germany, Saint Nicholas gives gifts to good girls and boys—and Krampus punishes the naughty ones. And Krampus would actually come to our house with Saint Nicholas—they were probably people from our apartment building. They were scary as shit, carrying chains and wearing horns, the devil side of Santa. I didn't know exactly what was going on when I was little, except that Krampus gave me chocolate. In my childish brain, this began an association with fear and sweets. I'm frightened, but there must be something good about all of this, because look at this candy!

Yes, strangers with candy made me who I am today. There was some logic to it from my upbringing, too. I was essentially raised at the opera, where there was mayhem and lust and war and dying, but I got snacks and naps and picture books. You take from something things that are already in your nature, and for me, I decided that there was a kind of magic in horror, an element that was like treasure if you were brave enough to get through to it.

For me, from a very young age, that treasure was food, preferably with sugar involved in its creation. Now that I'm a professional baker, that translates into creations, sometimes, that aren't completely comprehensible at first glance. Some of my cakes, well, you might not even be sure that they're cakes—at first. But if you're patient and trust that it is a cake? You'll get to enjoy it. Otherwise, you'll just walk away and never know.

I'm not the person who sits there and painstakingly carves

flowers from blocks of fondant, although I'm happy to eat a fondant-covered slice of cake. My focus is always on something that's slightly absurd or impossible—but I want it to be delicious. I want it to be a pastry that you don't want to put down.

At the same time, when you cook or bake, you know this is something someone's going to be ingesting. It's not just transitory, it's getting digested! Keeping a sense of humor about something that might seem gross or disturbing comes straight from Struwwelpeter.

Once, when I ran a bakery, someone ordered the cake we always made for baby showers. So I made the cake, which we always did in the shape of a big, pregnant belly—people loved it. When the customer came to pick it up, she said, "It's for my grandmother's eightieth birthday," and I realized that she had ordered the cake flavor—not the big belly! So they were waiting, and I knew what I had to do: perform a cake cesarean.

I was terrified (it was an expensive order!), but I had to get it done as quickly and beautifully as I could. But sometimes, in those moments, when you don't panic, things can be kind of transcendent. You cut right in, with the precision of a German children's book illustrator, and in the end, you've got something pretty sweet.

Gesine Bullock-Prado is a renowned pastry chef and author of the baking memoir My Life from Scratch *and the cookbooks* Sugar Baby, Pie It Forward, *and* Bake It Like You Mean It. *She is a regular guest on the* Today *show and the* Food Network.

KEITH CARRADINE

on *The Book of Daniel*
by E. L. Doctorow

"It made me want to tell a story, too"

I love to read, and read so much, but it was easy to know which book I'd choose. *The Book of Daniel* by E. L. Doctorow completely changed my life when I read it in 1972.

The Book of Daniel is about Julius and Ethel Rosenberg, who were executed in 1953 for crimes of treason against the United States. They had passed information about the atomic bomb to the Soviet Union. In the novel, Doctorow calls his characters Paul and Rochelle Isaacson. But his protagonist, and the reason the book hit me so deeply, is their son, Daniel.

It was the first time I read a book that turns something like that on its head, that took an event I remembered and considered it from a different angle—or at least it was the first time I realized I was reading a book like that. In 2015 we may not all remember how deeply divided this country was in the early 1970s, but it was an important time for me and I do remember how well I could relate to Daniel Isaacson, twenty-five in 1967 as the book opens, and how confusing it was then to separate the personal from the political and McCarthyism from Nixon's shenanigans.

Daniel is literally lost at the book's start, hitchhiking with his wife and baby. The whole thing wouldn't work at all if he were an apologist for his parents, but he's not. It wouldn't work, either, if he loathed his parents. Instead, Doctorow makes him conflicted. He's a sort of hippie who wants to fight the power, but he also lived through a hellish childhood where home was unstable and he and his sister got passed around to live in various places when his parents were in prison.

The things we do change other people. The things Daniel's parents did, whether they were wrong or right, no matter how much they believed in what they were doing, affected their children. *The Book of Daniel* may be fiction, but even if the Isaacsons did things that the historical Rosenbergs didn't do, that's still true. The book affected me so strongly that I wrote a song about it for my second album, *Lost and Found*. The song is "Homeless Eyes," and one of its lines is "This child knows the score."

I think so many children of the 1960s forgot that what they were doing would not just change the world but also affect their own children. Maybe it was because baby boomers had relatively stable and privileged childhoods compared to their parents. I don't know, but I do know that Doctorow's beautiful examination of how a baby boomer who did not have a stable or privileged childhood navigates the rest of his life, well, it made me want to tell a story, too.

Keith Carradine is an actor and musician who performed his hit 1975 song "I'm Easy" in the film Nashville. *Currently starring as President Conrad Dalton in the TV show* Madam Secretary, *Carradine is part of a legendary acting family that includes his daughter Martha Plimpton.*

MAUD CASEY

on *Man in the Holocene*

by Max Frisch

"Making sense of the world"

I recently moved to a new house and used the opportunity to apply Marie Kondo's *The Life-Changing Magic of Tidying Up*. Thinking about it, I realize that after all that tidying, I *only* have the books that have changed my life in my study. The whole idea with the tidying is boiling things down to the essentials that shape your life so that you can start making big decisions.

One of the books that shaped my life is *Man in the Holocene* by Max Frisch, a Swiss novelist. I just reread it to teach last spring, and I still read my fifteen-year-old copy from a second-hand bookstore, completely annotated with my scrawl. It's this strange, beautiful little book about an older man named Geiser who's been trapped in an Alpine valley in Switzerland because of an avalanche. He's growing increasingly panicked by his isolation and basically starts reading in order to keep himself sane.

Geiser has become fatigued by novels. He instead turns to nonfiction, especially books that are historical, about evolution and biology and geology. He's trying to understand himself in context—who am I in relation to the universe? As you follow the book, you begin to see how unconcerned with humankind the natural world is. There's a line about the way nature doesn't need Geiser's memory. Nature doesn't even need the term "Holocene Period." The novel is about the futility of making sense of the world, but also the beauty and clemency of trying.

This last rereading was my fifth, and whenever I read it to teach, it's an intensified kind of reading. The books you teach become part of the way you move through the world. In addition to the big questions and ideas of the novel, Frisch's style is just so formally inventive and weird that it blows my mind every time.

Frisch was an architect, and his expertise as a maker of structures shows everywhere in this structure made of words. He plays with the idea of what should go where. Could you put a window on the roof? Does a door always open the same way? What if a text itself were embedded in a dwelling? As Geiser is reading, he starts ripping pages out of books and putting them up on the wall of his house. It's as if he's starting to live inside of a book, just the way a reader does, but he also uses the pages in the collage Geiser is making to tell a story.

I once came across a description of the way the 1979 English edition was translated, and one of the things that struck me was that the German title is *Mann Erscheint im Holocene*, which translates as *Man Emerging in the Holocene*, or *Emergent Man in the Holocene*. Emergent, right? It's less static that way than with just the preposition. It made me think about the fact that we're unfinished. Mankind is still emerging.

When I teach this novel, there is usually a student who says,

"Wow, this is all so grim." But to me this book is so optimistic. Yes, it's incredibly stark and brutal. But there's a sort of peace to it as well. Geiser is gone from the narration at the end, but his clippings are there, the landscape is there, an owl is there. Our protagonist is gone, but his sensibility is still there. You feel that he's been absorbed into the universe in this kind of transcendent way because of a kind of humility. Peace. Finality.

The book that changed my life. It's an effective, simple question, but it really—it's a rare occasion, I think, that we are asked to stop in this swirl of our reading and think, "Okay, what is this whole thing about? How am I affected by the consciousness of others, these sensibilities I absorb as I read?"

Maud Casey is the author of The Man Who Walked Away, The Shape of Things to Come, *and* Genealogy, *as well as a collection of short stories,* Drastic. *Casey teaches at the University of Maryland and lives in Washington, DC.*

Rosanne Cash

on *Little House on the Prairie* by Laura Ingalls Wilder

"A template for the future"

At ten, I was a shy, chubby, nonathletic child with a very intense inner life. I asked my mom to drop me at the library on Saturdays, rather than find friends to play with.

On one of those Saturdays I discovered the *Little House* series by Laura Ingalls Wilder and it was one of the greatest things ever to happen to me. I entered a world where things were ordered, simple, and predictable. Laundry was on Monday. Ironing was on Tuesday. At certain times of the year, a pig was killed. Relatives came to visit. People made maple syrup.

These things soothed me. My childhood was so fantastically chaotic and unpredictable, with the complicating factors of drug addiction and fame in my father, and utter misery and sometimes hysteria in my mother. When Laura Ingalls Wilder wrote about Ma setting the table for dinner and how the light looked when it came through the window from the prairie, and how Pa played the fiddle in the evenings—it gave me the courage to face my own life and my own family. It gave me peace, and a template for the future.

I retreated into those books. I don't know that I had a conscious knowledge of what it was doing for me—the very ordering of my soul—but I felt it. Later, when I read the series to my own children, I realized what it had given me, and the pleasure of giving it to my children was just as acute and sweet.

I wanted to keep my copies pristine. Write in the margins? *Never!* Sacrilege! I did not race through these books. I savored them. I reread passages over and over. I still think of scenes from the series. *The Long Winter* has become my favorite over time. Now that I'm writing books, too, I can see that Ingalls Wilder's prose has had an effect on my own. Her meticulously careful observation of a scene, a person, the light, the feel of the cashmere, the sound of the fiddle, the color of Mary's eyes, the print of the tablecloth, the shock on baby Grace's face when she is reprimanded. All those tiny observations made an enormous impact on me. I endeavor to be that careful.

Laura's steadfastness pleases me so much. I go back to the books and there she is, same as ever. It's all still happening. When I read the series to my son, when he was about eight, and who is now sixteen, he was just as riveted as I was the first time I encountered the series. He loved *The Long Winter* just as much as me. The only things he resisted were the "peripheral" stories of Almanzo's childhood and Rose's story. I was a little disappointed, but realized he's even more of a purist than me.

Rosanne Cash is an American singer-songwriter and author. She is the eldest daughter of the late country music singer Johnny Cash and his first wife, Vivian Liberto Cash Distin. Her 2010 memoir, Composed, *details her upbringing and her launch as a musician.*

OTIS CHANDLER

on *Dune* by Frank Herbert

"Full of big ideas"

I found Frank Herbert's *Dune* series on my father's bookshelf when I was in junior high—and I've probably read it three times (it's a big series) since then.

Dune grabs you and doesn't let go. It's full of big ideas about spirituality, religion, and politics. I loved the spiritual ideas the best, especially the philosophies and practices of the prana-bindu training of the Bene Gesserit. Paul, the main character, learns these and then builds on them. The notion that human beings could improve themselves to such a degree enthralled me. It still does. I also must admit that I still chant (in my mind) the Litany Against Fear whenever I am afraid: "I will not fear. Fear is the mind-killer. . ."

Herbert's books helped me in two ways. First, they gave me a better understanding of the world and its complexities, whether those are political, religious, psychological—it showed me at a young age that things could rarely be reduced to slogans or quaint sayings. Second, the spiritual concepts he writes about have served me my entire life to keep calm in moments of stress or distress.

Between big moments in my life, I reread *Dune*, most recently about two years ago, which was the first time I read it digitally. I have become addicted to reading digitally so that I can save my highlights and quotes, and I was interested to see what I might save and find from these books this time around. (You can find some of the quotes I've shared publicly in my Goodreads review.)

One thing I realized after the last rereading was how seemingly tailored the book is to the issues in the Middle East in the 1970s, and how most of those issues remain the same today yet are slightly different, which makes for interesting conversations with newer readers of *Dune*. One thing is certain though: oil remains a scant resource that still controls our world. I am hopeful we will change that in my lifetime.

I still have my original copy, which was a copy I got from my father. It is therefore precious to me, as I lost my father many years ago. It is dog-eared and old but in decent shape. *Dune* also inspires me to be a better leader. Seeing Goodreads grow from a handful of employees to over one hundred today (and still growing!) has come with a lot of leadership challenges, but I've learned that humans really can continue to improve, and that one of the best ways to do that is through encouraging teamwork.

Otis Chandler is the founder and CEO of Goodreads. He spends his time thinking about the future of reading. He's an entrepreneur, a product person, a book lover, a surfer, and a geek.

Ron Charles

on *Straight Man*
by Richard Russo

"It completely redirected my life"

For about five years, I taught English at a St. Louis prep school. A student's mother called me one day and said I could be doing more with my life, which is kind of an offensive thing to say, really. I think she believed teaching high school in the Midwest was not ambitious enough. Maybe she called a lot of us on the faculty, because one of my colleagues was Jon Hamm. You may have heard of him.

But I took her advice, maybe because I, too, thought I should be doing something else. Not something better. Just something different. Teaching was the most important and noble and enjoyable thing I ever did, but I was worn down by grading papers.

Since I taught English, I thought I might try writing a book review, but I didn't know anything about it at all. But I'd been teaching for a while, which meant I had a lot of experience introducing books to a reluctant audience. So I went to a giant independent bookstore in St. Louis called Library, Ltd. (It's gone now, like so many others.) There was a little table of new books up front, and I saw one that was about an English teacher, by an author I'd never heard of, and this will show you how out of the loop I was on books and publishing: it was *Straight Man*, by Richard Russo.

So I read it, wrote up eight hundred words, and sent it off to the only newspaper book section I had any sort of "in" with, which was through a friend at the *Christian Science Monitor*. She passed it along to the books editor, who bought it and asked for more. For eight or nine months, I would go to the bookstore, poke around on the "New Books" table, choose something, and send in a review. A little more than half the time, the editor bought them.

But then he wrote and said he couldn't accept any more reviews because he was changing jobs and didn't want to leave any half-finished assignments for his successor. I wrote back and asked if they would consider me for the job, and he responded that they already had somebody.

So of course I applied. To the managing editor. Unbeknownst to me, I had had his daughter as a student years before, so he recognized my name and pushed my application through. They hired me, and I moved my family to Boston.

Straight Man wasn't a book that changed my life just because I loved it. It physically changed my life! It completely redirected my life. I don't think you'll find anyone who was more changed by a book.

Let me say, too, that Russo is a hero of mine. I've reviewed several of his books since, and I think he's one of our great American writers. He's funny, he has just the right touch of sentimentality, and he understands people.

Every week for eighteen years now, I've written a review:

snappy opening, plot description, critical commentary, a few characteristic quotes, sign off. And it's agony every week; I just sweat it out. But now, at least, I get to choose which books I review, and I choose books I expect to like. That brings us back to *Straight Man*, I guess. I chose a book I thought I'd like, and I did, and I conveyed what I liked to an editor.

That's basically our job as critics, right? Figuring out how to rephrase the phrase "This is really, really good." Newspaper readers overwhelmingly prefer to read positive reviews, which, I know, raises all kinds of complicated critical questions, but I don't blame them. Of course, they want to know which books they should read instead of which books they should not read— because they're not going to read most books, anyhow.

The world in which I became a book reviewer is, for all intents and purposes, gone. The newspaper industry is completely different now. When I left the *Monitor*, fearing it was going to close, I could barely apply fast enough as book sections shut down around the country. Maybe I should be doing something else with my life. Time to call Jon Hamm. . . .

Ron Charles is the editor of the Washington Post Book World.

ALEXANDER CHEE

on *The Quest for Christa T.*
by Christa Wolf

"At home embracing contradiction"

The book that changed my life wound up changing it personally and professionally, while still being very much of its time, which was my time, too, in a way: the 1980s. It was *The Quest for Christa T.* by Christa Wolf.

I was just incredibly taken with the voice of that narrator, the mix of cold severity with which she regards herself, and the commitment that her character has to her own sexuality. It's this really interesting mix of aesthetics: the spare modernity of Eastern Europe behind the Iron Curtain combined with eroticism. It was a really powerful sense of recognition for me. I felt this need to try to write like that.

Wolf and other authors I love—Jean Rhys, Marguerite Yourcenar—have that kind of narrator who is pushing hard into their own experience to understand a self in relation to the world.

It was very much what I have wound up doing, although I didn't see the connection at the time.

I'm drawn to stories about exile, about places that mean something to a person or a character even after—especially after—they leave those places. It was something I was also doing at the time. I spent a lot of my childhood leaving places, and even, technically, before that, since my mother was pregnant with me when my parents moved from one continent to another. I definitely grew up with this notion of despair. It's something that haunted me for a long time and I would say still haunts me.

At the same time—I was around nineteen when I read Wolf—I was learning about my sexual nature, about the power of being attracted to men and being attractive to men and what I wanted to do with that. In the 1980s, there was a lot of promise and hopefulness in the gay community, but there was also sickness, death, and a lot of doors closed to us.

That heightened the sense I already had of not quite belonging to any group, as well as observing the negotiation marginalized groups make with the dominant ones around them. But it wasn't just about gender identity and sexual politics for me, any more than it was for Wolf. It was also about figuring out how any individual fits into any collective, how to hold on to what is most precious to you while maintaining ties to the world, ties that you don't necessarily want to sever just because the world isn't what you wish it could be.

My copy of *The Quest for Christa T.* came from a friend who had gone to study in Berlin for a year and had been absolutely changed by it. She was, in a sense, my own Christa T., the friend who was always somehow bolder and more resolutely determined to be herself no matter what. And she still is, and she still lives in

Berlin, and she still works completely freelance—but she recently married, and she was the last person I thought would ever do that. I still have the book, and it doesn't have any annotations in it at all. I was scolded as a child if I made marks in books. It's a powerful stigma for me now. I still can't write in the margins. That's funny, right? I'm talking about living in margins, but I find it difficult to write in them.

My friend's decision to marry made me think again about Wolf's novel, and I realize that the negotiations we make with restrictions and boundaries might be symbolized by a particular era in history, or an era in our own lives. That era, or a certain rule, might not keep changing—but the ones in our heads do. In the decades since I first read *The Quest for Christa T.*, I've marveled at how that book affected me then. Now I know that it's still affecting me, that I'm still negotiating and still changing. It's fitting that Wolf was buried in a cemetery that's right on the old divide between East and West Berlin. I feel like her, like a person most at home embracing contradiction.

Alexander Chee, author of Edinburgh, *was born in Rhode Island and raised in South Korea, Guam, and Maine. His second novel,* The Queen of the Night, *will be released by Houghton Mifflin Harcourt in February 2016.*

ALAN CHEUSE

on *Ulysses*
by James Joyce

"My working bible"

The first book that influenced me was the King James Bible—
that language! It just seeps into your consciousness.

The second book that hit me hard was one that I stumbled
on completely by accident. I was about twelve, so this must have
been 1952 or so, and I had been reading a lot of adventure books.
There was a reading contest at my local library, and I kept going
in to take out more books so I could win the contest, and every
time I entered the library there was a display of new books. One
of them had a great title—*Invisible Man*. I finally took it out because I thought, "Wow, here's a book about an invisible man," and
I wanted to find out what made him invisible.

Of course, this was Ralph Ellison's *Invisible Man*, which had
nothing to do with supernatural disappearance. But I read the first
page, then the second, and I was hooked. By the time the contest
was over, I don't think I had even gotten past the first chapter of

Ellison, because the language was so rich and resonant—a lot like the King James Bible, really. That was the first serious novel I ever read.

But the book that has changed my life is *Ulysses* by James Joyce. That's my working bible. It's a compendium of every narrative technique ever. Through a fantastic combination of circumstances I recently met a Joyce aficionado who actually has assembled a library on the author, and I was given the opportunity to hold and look at a manuscript of the novel. He also showed me a signed first edition of *Finnegans Wake* and a first edition of *Ulysses*. It's the most extraordinary thing that's happened to me in a long time. One of the closest things to a religious experience, for sure.

It's one of the books that most people would consider to be among the most difficult in the English language—yet I've found, along the way, that it often strikes a chord with people who are utterly nonliterary, which is not meant to sound snobbish. Joyce connects to the things that we all share; he has this radical acceptance and enjoyment of life. Yet he holds to a higher standard, much like Melville does in *Moby-Dick*. In fact, for me, *Moby-Dick* stands between the Bible and *Ulysses*.

I teach *Ulysses* as often as I can, but not as often as I would like. I tend to teach his stories, because it's easier to get students to read those rather than one of the novels. But it's such a touchstone for me. I'm about to leave for the West Coast, which is a geographical touchstone for me, and here's how those two things are connected: When I saw the Pacific Coast for the first time, years ago, I realized that there was so much more to be discovered. So much possibility. Every time I pick up *Ulysses*, I think about that, how Joyce came after so many masters, so many times when someone said, "There is nothing left to be written," or "There is nothing more to be done with the novel," and yet he found the possibilities.

Alan Cheuse was an American academic, critic, and writer who re-viewed books for NPR's All Things Considered *for thirty years until his death in 2015.*

Caldecot Chubb

on *The Marriage of Heaven and Hell*
by William Blake

"We're all in the story business"

At a time in my life when it seemed inconceivable that the story I had been told about the way the world is could actually be accurate, William Blake's poem *The Marriage of Heaven and Hell* was very attractive. I'd been raised in the Episcopal Church, and Blake's notions about how human life is governed, how Lucifer is the bringer of light—these were attractive concepts when I was twenty-one.

The most important parts of it are, of course, the proverbs of hell and the three principles, his notion of what governed human morals when the dogma of religion fails. Blake writing, "As I went walking among the fires of hell . . . ," made a great deal of sense to me, and that still does, as a way of understanding human nature in its most poetic and brutal sense, a way that seemed to be correct. I know what it means to say, "The cut worm forgives the plow." Most moral guidance is dangerous, in my opinion, but

Blake's moral guidance seemed quite sensible. And sensitive.

I work both in the art business and in the movie business. In both I have found it instructive to consider the vagaries of human nature through Blake's lens. It's dangerous to think that the road of excess leads to the palace of wisdom, but there's truth to it, too. Part of what I do as a producer is to work with writers and read scripts and decide how they might accord better with any number of things, from human connection to commercial viability. I have learned that true improvement makes straight roads, but crooked roads are the roads to genius. Straight roads might be better, or more efficient, but they don't necessarily delight.

Yes, Blake was a madman, and I find it humorous that I am taking moral instruction from someone who was so clearly troubled, but it has been consistently valuable and inspiring and useful to me. I dropped out of college because, as Blake says, "the tigers of wrath are better than the horses of instruction," and while I sometimes regret that choice, I find myself in a business where instinct is extremely important.

So I do go back and read *The Marriage of Heaven and Hell;* I just did so the other day because I'm about to go and teach a semester at the University of North Carolina School of the Arts. I'm teaching about stories, and I was thinking about how to do that. I might have one class write stories about specific morals.

One of the things young people in the movie business need is an understanding of stories: How to tell them. How to identify their elements. How to capture and keep someone's attention. I want them to tell a lot of stories, and the best way to get an intuitive feel for story is to read a lot. How many of them are actually going to make a living in the movie business? Not many, but all of them are going to have to get along in life, and most of life is about creating resonant narratives. That's how you persuade people, instruct people, pitch people, and so on. Few things drive me more crazy than the current locution of "content." One way or another, we're all in the story business.

Caldecot Chubb is a film and television producer whose notable projects include Eve's Bayou, Hoffa, Appaloosa, The Crow, *and* Good Morning, Babylon.

SOFIA COPPOLA

on *The Virgin Suicides*
by Jeffrey Eugenides

"I wanted to protect what I loved about the book"

A friend told me about *The Virgin Suicides* by Jeffrey Eugenides, and I liked the cover—a close-up of blond hair unspooling on the ground.

It made me want to direct a movie, because I wanted to adapt this book. So it led to my career as a director. I had an idea of how I thought it should be done as a film, and I heard someone else was trying to do that—and I thought they were doing it wrong. I wanted to protect what I loved about the book.

The Virgin Suicides was the first contemporary novel I had read that I felt was a classic. I do love an obsessive love story, which you could probably tell from a list of my other favorite books: *Anna Karenina, Madame Bovary, Sentimental Education, Of Human Bondage,* and *Lolita.*

I started reading avidly around the time I was eleven, when I found *A Wrinkle in Time* and couldn't put it down. It was the same way with Eugenides. I read all the way through, staying up late, and then I reread it straight through, making a lot of notes with a fluorescent pink pencil. That copy is still on my bookshelf and probably always will be. I mean, I don't reread books, because I feel like there are so many classics I haven't gotten to yet.

That's why, I'm sure, *The Virgin Suicides* remains a beloved book. It has that engrossing feel, the feeling that you can't possibly do anything else until you know the end of the story.

Sofia Coppola is a film director, screenwriter, producer, and actor. She directed The Virgin Suicides *and* Lost in Translation, *winning an Oscar for the latter.*

CAT CORA

on *The Art of Eating*
by M. F. K. Fisher

"You can nearly smell it right from the page"

My reading goes across all genres—mystery, self-help, something deeper—sometimes I have three books going at once. I looked back at my library, which is mostly on my tablet these days, to tell you the truth, and I thought, "Wow, I read a lot!"

I'm a voracious reader and I always have been. My parents were both academics, and there were always books around. I remember having all of the Nancy Drew mysteries as the first books of my own, and I'm trying to instill the power of reading as an escape and a means to education in all four of my boys. My wife and I have always read to them, since they were babies, and I want them to have that wonderful journey, that adventure, that you have when you're reading.

I grew up reading the "normal" great books: Steinbeck, Hemingway, books like that. We lived in Jackson, Mississippi, so I also went through a big Southern literature and writers period.

I loved Eudora Welty, and I even got to meet her a few times and get books signed by her. My mother actually is a docent at the garden of her house now. We're big fans. Willie Morris, too. I read everything, but as I got older, I started choosing books a little more carefully based on my own individual interests instead of my family's interests, my geographical context, all that stuff.

So when I was in college, I read *The Art of Eating* by M. F. K. Fisher. It's so important to me. For a long time I required anyone who worked for me, every sous chef, to read that book. It's so insightful. She's not even writing about food. She's writing about warmth and comfort and hunger and all those things.

I remember one story in which she talks about tangerines and she put them on the heater to dry them a little bit before she ate them, and she describes the scent in the room. It's amazing. I love thinking about that intense citrus aroma. Of course, she is also, in that moment, in those lines, explaining the intensity of her longing for sunshine in a cold winter in France, her bare-bones housing, and how weird it is that the modern world lets us eat something exotic out of season and context.

Whatever it is that she writes about—wine, bread, cheese, vegetables—she takes those things that people take for granted in so many ways, she gives a way of looking at food. You think you have a passion for food? Let's go deeper. That's why I wanted my cooks to read Fisher's work. She talks about broiling or frying or baking this or that, but no matter what kind of preparation she's involved in, you can nearly smell it right from the page.

I've just written a memoir, *Cooking as Fast as I Can*. It's pretty honest, and sometimes raw, and I hope it has some inspiration in it for people who have experienced some of the same things I have in my life. I know it's not anything like M. F. K. Fisher's writing, and I'm not trying to write that way. But her writing inspired me to take time and tell my own story, because I know how much her story encouraged me to look at the things I'm most passionate about in a new way.

In addition to being a celebrated chef, Cat Cora is an accomplished lifestyle entrepreneur, author, restaurateur, contributing editor, and television personality. Her memoir Cooking as Fast as I Can *was released in 2015.*

Douglas Coupland

on *The Andy Warhol Diaries*

"Words can be art supplies"

Unlike some novelists, I went to art school, not university. I was reading, but I was a visual artist, but it was an interesting historical moment as text was starting to become art—artists like Jenny Holzer and Barbara Kruger, say.

Warhol died in 1987 and in 1989 I bought a posthumously printed copy of *The Andy Warhol Diaries*, because—basically, I missed him and missed his being in the world.

Warhol began keeping a diary because the Republicans put him on their tax shit list. Anti-Nixon posters made a huge amount of money for the Democrats, so Warhol was always being audited. What began as a daily tally of events and receipts quickly morphed into a social history of New York society during its golden years. His cowriter and accomplice was Pat Hackett, and they spoke every morning for over a decade.

The diary entries were a sort of text version of Warhol's famous brown-box "time capsules," cardboard boxes where he put everything he received in the course of a day: party invites, photos, free samples, coffee cans—Warhol was a borderline hoarder. All of the names from that era figure prominently in the diaries: Halston, Liza Minnelli, Bianca Jagger—the diaries are sort of an early form of Twitter.

It fascinated me to learn that no matter where he was (often overseas), Warhol never missed his daily diary calls with Pat Hackett. Warhol came from poor origins and was often frugal and was always looking for new ways to finance his expansive art and media career. The diaries became a way of monetizing his life, which is funny and ironic. Warhol was an interesting permission giver in that he showed that art could be made out of words. Words can be art supplies. That changed my life. These days I consider myself a visual artist more than a writer.

I think that people tend to be either visual thinkers or verbal thinkers. I'm both and I have trouble being around people who are only one or the other. Warhol was definitely both, which helps explain his enduring appeal, many decades past his fifteen minutes.

Although I've published some novels, I am back to working primarily on nontextual visual art. I'd hope that if a person enjoys my books, they'll take a look at my online world and then become interested in the many museum and gallery projects I'm involved with.

Douglas Coupland is a Canadian novelist, visual artist, and designer. His first novel, in 1991, was Generation X. *He has published thirteen novels, a collection of short stories, seven nonfiction books, and a number of dramatic works and screenplays for stage, film, and television.*

PETER COYOTE

on *The Odyssey*
by Homer

"A complex panoply of human values"

I've read every translation of Homer's *Odyssey* in English. Even the one by Alexander Pope in rhyming couplets! Every single one, because it's such a powerful work.

I first read the poem in high school, and there was something so fundamental about the story to me, something so powerful. Odysseus was such a different hero. He was unreliable. He wasn't altogether good. He represented a complex panoply of human values. This story, coming out of an oral tradition, represented a completely different way of looking at what makes someone important to a culture.

It seized my imagination. It had everything. War, money, magic, spying, metaphors; I mean, how many times in your life have you mentioned "caught between the Scylla and Charybdis"? How many times have we referred to males as "pigs"? "The wine-dark sea," "rosy-fingered dawn," all of this comes to us from

Homer. There's great adventure, and there's also great failure, dark episodes that show us people in ancient Greece weren't just sitting around watching sitcom reruns on Hulu.

I'm not sure which translation I read in high school, but it was probably Chapman's, in that earwormlike iambic pentameter. Robert Fitzgerald's came out when I was in college, and I loved it; even after Albert Cook's came out, I preferred Fitzgerald's. I've also read Fagles, Lombardo, and Mandelbaum, but I think my favorite is Richmond Lattimore's from 1967. That's because, as far as I can tell from reading and from hearing critical reviews, it comes closest to sounding like Homer: "Tell me, Muse, of the man of many ways . . ."

My most recent reading was about four or five years ago, after hearing this spoken-word performance of *The Odyssey*. I know I'll read it again, because I always find something new to focus on when I do. This last time, I was really captivated by what an ass Odysseus is when he gets home, and how he has to get to the point where he can say "I want nothing. I fear nothing. I am free."

At certain times in my life, like when I was part of [the 1960s anarchist theater collective] the Diggers, I was trying to be unencumbered, although that doesn't mean there weren't distinct periods of decadence and experimentation. As I've gotten older, my priority has always been to stay as free as possible to pursue whatever creative project I could imagine, and for that you need to keep a pipeline open to your imagination. The richer the art and literature that pump into that pipeline, the better that project will be.

Books like *The Odyssey*, *The Iliad*, and *Anna Karenina*, those books give you something different at every stage of your life. They also serve as high-water marks for what we can achieve when we stay open to all that the world has to offer. I'm never going to be Homer, or Tolstoy, but I can keep writing and I'm working on a new novel at the moment, as well as reading as much as I can.

Peter Coyote is an American actor, author, director, screenwriter, and narrator of films, theater, television, and audiobooks. He won a Pushcart Prize for "Carla's Story" in 1994. His memoir, The Rainman's Third Cure: An Irregular Education, *was published by Counterpoint Press in 2015.*

LIEUTENANT GENERAL FLORA DARPINO

US Army Judge Advocate General

on *The Best American Short Stories 2009*

"It's about the human dimension"

Reading has always been very important to me, but reading has also always been "for the season." By that I mean, for instance, when my kids were little and my life was as incredibly busy at home as at work, I always read essays or short stories. I knew that I couldn't devote myself to a full-length novel.

That's when I started picking up the collections *The Best American Short Stories*, *The Best American Essays*, and so forth. I found, for that point in my life, I could read things of that length. I could read something no matter how exhausted I was. I could read one short story and get my fix. Since those collections include work from many different writers, you get all these different styles, so

I never felt that I was getting stuck finishing twenty stories by a writer I found I didn't like.

I found this important during another period of my life, too, during my two overseas deployments during the Iraq War. I knew I was going to be in the same situation as I had been when I was a new mother. I wouldn't be able to read a full-length book—not just because I couldn't read for hours at a time, but because trying to pick up a sustained, intense prose work would be impossible. I allowed myself one big book on the flight over—*Seabiscuit* by Laura Hillenbrand—and one book on the flight home—*Bridge of Sighs* by Richard Russo.

But once I got there, I knew I wasn't going to be able to do that. So I brought more short story collections. I would read them before going to bed at night as my wind-down from the duty day.

Part of what was so important to me about short stories was I knew I could complete them. You know when you read a novel, you get so involved in the story and its characters as they tumble across the page and the author weaves that web you try to discern, all of those things that you absolutely love about reading a book? You can't do that when you're deployed and you don't see an end in sight. Deployment feels continuous. You are the tumbling character. That web is your life.

With a short story to read, and a short story of the same type as the books I enjoy, I could have all of the things I love about literature—and I could accomplish something. I would lie on my cot and look at how many pages I'd just finished and think, "I accomplished something today." Everything else could've gone wrong.

Now that I'm back in the United States, I've become a big gardener. After I run in the morning, as I see our house, I can see something I've accomplished. And sometimes that's important.

When all you deal with in the day are problems, to actually have something you've completed—that's resolution. I don't know. It's comforting. I don't know how else to put it. It reminds you where you started, where you come from. It reminds you of home.

People often say to me, "Are you reading any good military history?" And the answer is no. I'll read a book on a region that I'm going to, I'll read historical fiction about the military, but I don't spend time reading actual military history books because, to me, it's about the human dimension. The books I choose, the literature I choose, lay out the human dimension of the military.

Lieutenant General Flora Darpino is the judge advocate general of the United States Army and the first woman to hold that position.

KENNETH C. DAVIS

on *A Portrait of the Artist as a Young Man*
by James Joyce

"We are fascinated by stories"

Choosing which book changed my life is such a difficult question for me as a historian, because I think of myself as a person who read history and was profoundly influenced by that. But I also think of myself as a writer first, and if I had to say which writer influenced me the most, it would be James Joyce and his novel *A Portrait of the Artist as a Young Man.*

Like most of the writers you're talking to, I was a huge reader as a child, and also a devoted library goer as a child. We did not have a bookstore in the town I grew up in, which is Mount Vernon, New York, the hometown of a guy named E. B. White. Nobody made a big deal of that, but we were all secretly very proud of it. Instead of a bookstore, we had a magnificent public library, which was a Carnegie library, a true temple to books and learning.

I remember you went to the bottom floor, the children's room, and there was this magnificent grand staircase that went up to the second floor, which was the adult room and the reference room. The day that you could get an adult library card was such a rite of passage.

I was a history bug, which is not surprising, so it was not until college that I actually read *A Portrait of the Artist as a Young Man*. I did not envision myself as a writer, because that notion was about as far removed as becoming an astronaut or a brain surgeon. Growing up in the 1960s, you might see writers on TV occasionally. But Truman Capote, Gore Vidal, and Jacqueline Susann, to name three writers who were on TV often, were another kind of celebrity. I had never met a writer. No writers ever visited my classrooms.

There's really something important I think about people understanding that there is a person behind these books, and I didn't really make that connection for a very, very long time.

Joyce's book really opened my eye up, my mind up, to the idea of the writer as the artist and creator, that a human being had done this. I remember actually having to do a reading in a college class of a section of a book, and I had actually chosen a very memorable scene from *A Portrait of the Artist* that is usually called "the bird girl scene," where Stephen, the narrator, is watching this young woman standing on the beach. It's this incredible moment that's erotic and artistic and worshipful all rolled into one, as Joyce can be. I mean, that really did it for me. It's that you can find a way to put these words together that makes sense of a much bigger picture—to get at truth.

I still reread the book regularly, and I often reread that scene in particular because, you know, you might have one book in your life that's important, but then you have one scene in one book that's important. And that's it for me. It's perhaps one of the finest pieces of writing that spoke to me in my entire life. And

I can probably come up with other books that have important passages and significant passages, but that moment is it.

Any great writers, whether fiction or nonfiction, share two things. They're great storytellers, and they use the stories they tell to try to make sense of the world, which is to say we all tell stories to get at the truth. We are fascinated by stories. That's why we created myths, says the historian in me, sacred stories that help us make sense of the world.

Great writing ultimately uses a great story to tell us a great truth. When you combine those things, you have great art, I think. *A Portrait of the Artist as a Young Man* by James Joyce is definitely great art, something that through the power of the written word makes you see a glimpse of truth for which you've forgotten to ask. (I'm paraphrasing Joseph Conrad here, another writer who created art.) And I think that's the greatest aspiration any writer can have.

Kenneth C. Davis is the author of Don't Know Much About History, *which spent thirty-five consecutive weeks on the* New York Times *bestseller list and gave rise to the* Don't Know Much About *series of books and audiobooks, which has a combined in-print total of some 4.7 million copies. His latest book is* The Hidden History of America at War: Untold Tales from Yorktown to Fallujah.

TOM DAVIS

on *The Emerging Republican Majority*
by Kevin Phillips

"Collaboration and compromise"

As a kid, I followed statistics. I knew I wanted a political career.

In high school, I became a congressional page and got a taste of life on the Hill. During my years at Amherst College, I became intrigued with political parties and in 1968 read Kevin Phillips's *The Emerging Republican Majority*. Every page I read was just wow, wow, wow. I got to meet Phillips and then worked in the Nixon White House, which completely refocused my attitude toward elections and politics.

What I found so exciting about the book was its description of electoral coalitions, how they could reconstitute themselves, then swing back to a new level. I basically had the book memorized. Although it's dated now, it taught me to focus on big-picture issues that politicians too often neglect because they're looking at micro pictures—and therefore, they do not understand the macro view.

Phillips explained Nixon's 1968 win and what the Republican Party was doing right in the realm of presidential politics. Even though no one talks about the "Southern Strategy" anymore, it's still interesting to think about how the GOP realigned in order to bring in many groups of voters that had long been loyal to the Democratic Party. (By the way, Phillips also coined the term "Sun Belt," which has a lot less to do with politics now and a lot more with retirement!)

Last year I published a book with my former House colleague Martin Frost, *The Partisan Divide: Congress in Crisis*. Martin is a lifelong Democrat and I am a lifelong Republican, but in our combined four decades of congressional service, we each chaired our respective party campaign committees, and we learned a great deal about how to reach out across the aisle to get things done. I'm really proud of the blurbs we received from people like President Carter, Representative Pelosi, Donna Brazile, and many others, not necessarily because of their stature and experience (all of which is amazing), but because they come from different sides of the aisle and many different political perspectives. All of them understand that solutions won't come from taking our toys and heading home, but from dialogue, listening, and a commitment to what's best for our country.

The book that changed my life may be focused on one political party, but I am a firm believer that collaboration and compromise get more done than adhering to rigid partisan behavior.

Tom Davis served as a representative (R-VA) in Congress from 1994 to 2014. He is currently the director of federal government affairs for Deloitte LLP.

NELSON DEMILLE

on *Atlas Shrugged*
by Ayn Rand

"I wouldn't be the person I am today"

In college, I was a political science major, reading all of the usual texts. But all of it seemed derivative to me. *Atlas Shrugged* by Ayn Rand, on the other hand, raised issues about individualism that really spoke to me. It's kind of an iconoclastic novel. It's not the best-written book, and she was Russian originally, so it goes on and on and on and on. . . .

But Rand was an original thinker. Her philosophy of objectivism was something I'd never heard before. I'd been brought up a good Catholic boy and her rejection of religion was a little hard to swallow, although I understood her rejection of collectivism, which has something in common with religion, of course.

Objectivism is all about the virtues of selfishness, about not being your brother's keeper. The individual is responsible for himself and no one else. I don't totally buy what she said, but it did affect my thinking and my way of life. Before I give to a charity, for example, I think, "Is this really the best use of my money?"

I give money away when it has to do with children. A child with leukemia did not choose to have that disease. But if it's a charity for drug abusers? Well, you've made your choice. Virtually all of my charitable giving is directed toward children.

On the business end, it's the same thing. I tend to look at every proposition and say, what's in this for me? Of course, if helping someone else is also going to help you, if raising someone up is going to make a difference for you? By all means.

If more of us thought this way, it might not be a perfect society. I think, though, that it would eliminate some of the victim culture we have today, where everyone's the victim of something. I think more of us taking responsibility for our own well-being would make us feel more pride in our own achievements.

In a novel, you can create the world that Rand does in *Atlas Shrugged*, you can create a cautionary tale about where we might end up if we don't change our ways. I read the book when I was twenty, and then again when I was thirty, and for many years I subscribed to the *Objectivist Newsletter*. I think that the objectivist philosophy morphed over time, and it's not necessarily something I completely subscribe to. But Ayn Rand was not a conservative. She was a revolutionary. Revolutionaries, we all know, don't always have all of the practical, logistical points worked out. They have a vision, an idea, and Rand's has certainly lasted and continues to fascinate people. Young people still read it, it's still taught.

And my protagonists are always individualists. They may not be objectivists, but reading *Atlas Shrugged* gives us a new perspective, a refugee's perspective, on the American Dream: individual freedom, nonreliance on government, the pursuit of happiness. I believe in people reaching their maximum potential, and I think

Rand saw that, too. *Atlas Shrugged* isn't the best book I've ever read. It isn't a perfect book. However, it changed the way I think about how I function as a citizen. If I hadn't read it, I wouldn't be the person I am today.

Nelson DeMille's latest of more than two dozen novels is Radiant Angel. *A native of Long Island and a US Army veteran of the Vietnam War, he lives with his wife and son in Garden City, New York.*

LIZA DONNELLY

on *A Room of One's Own*
by Virginia Woolf

"People are always struggling with their lives"

Recently, I published a cartoon in which one woman says to another: "I've found a room of my own and it's between my ears." If you're a woman and you're an artist, you have to try to disconnect yourself from social pressures and find out who you really are, because we are constantly being told we have to act/be/look/speak/write/draw a certain way.

Virginia Woolf's *A Room of One's Own* spoke to me when I first read it, because she wrote about feminism and creativity, a subject that fascinated me. She consolidated and distilled a lot of what I've been thinking about for years. I didn't read the book until later in life, unlike many who read it in college, when I was asked to teach a women's studies course at Vassar College and it was on the curriculum. Woolf writes of the importance for women to have creative space and economic freedom in order to write, in order to truly find an artistic voice. This struck a nerve for me.

The book is one of a series of lectures that Woolf delivered to young women in university. Woolf advises patience as a creative, that it takes work and time to find your voice. I found this somewhat validating, even though by then, of course, I had already found a certain voice—but the search is ongoing. Woolf connects creativity and being a woman, a theme I had been exploring for the past ten years and a central theme of the book that I'm working on now, too. There are problems and difficulties for women who want to live as artists that are still gendered.

One of them, which Woolf realized, is that there is no such thing as a "woman cartoonist" or a "woman writer." There's not a particular style or way of doing any art that is specific to gender. But not only do women find it difficult to find their voice as a person within a society that presumes them to conform, the standards for what has typically been considered "good" come from work that has been made and judged by men. It's one of the reasons Dorothy Parker had difficulties; she wrote short stories, and the powers that be, who were male, privileged novels over stories. In her day, she was not considered a "serious writer" in the same way Hemingway was.

When I read *A Room of One's Own*, I remembered what it was like for me in my early twenties when I was trying to break into *The New Yorker*. I didn't find it easy. It's always difficult getting into *The New Yorker*! At that time, a book I found very important was Doris Lessing's *The Golden Notebook*, which showed me that I wasn't alone. Simply put, Lessing showed me that people —particularly other women—are always struggling with their lives, all different pieces of their lives.

Woolf didn't minimize the struggle. She pointed out that here's what you need if you are going to find your true voice as a person, here's how you can be a creative person instead of a gender that is unjustly being seen as secondary. Carol Gilligan's *In a Different Voice* was important for me in my young professional life, too, in considering how women's brains work, and that if they do work differently—I don't like to ghettoize women—the important thing to know is that you need to write about what's important to you. Don't write what society is telling you to write about, don't be who others want you to be. Write about what you think you need to write about.

Here's an example. My mother loved James Thurber and she loved *The New Yorker*. When I was around seven I would trace the drawings in *The Thurber Carnival*. I was pulled in by their simplicity and I was trying to connect with my mother, trying to make her laugh.

But Thurber—when he drew women they were either terrifying battleaxes or demure flowering things. These women confused me! From the 1940s until the 1970s, a large percentage of the cartoons in *The New Yorker* were male-centric. It was difficult to find a nuanced view of women; the humor was often derived by very stereotypical representations. And the cartoons were almost all drawn by men.

Fortunately, Lee Lorenz opened things up when he became the magazine's art editor in the 1970s, and published cartoonists like me, Nurit Karlin, Roz Chast, and Victoria Roberts. There had been women cartoonists in the magazine's early years, in the 1920s and '30s, but with the second wave of feminism, we were returning. We were finding our voices and riding a cultural wave of freedom of creativity—a loosening of the strictures of society—that had also briefly existed for women around the time Virginia Woolf published *A Room Of One's Own*. But it is ongoing. Finding, expressing, and maintaining one's creative voice is, I have found, an unending struggle.

Liza Donnelly has been a cartoonist for The New Yorker *for over thirty years. When she started, she was one of only three women cartoonists being published by the magazine at that time. Ms. Donnelly is the author of sixteen books, and her writing and cartoons have been published in many other publications, both here and abroad. Ms. Donnelly is an accomplished public speaker, and delivered a very popular TED talk on the subject of women and creativity that was translated into thirty-eight languages and viewed over a million times. She is a cultural envoy for the US State Department, and in 2014 received an honorary doctorate from the University of Connecticut for her work in women's rights and peace.*

DAVE EGGERS

on *Herzog*
by Saul Bellow

"How much any one sentence can do"

Saul Bellow's *Herzog* comes to mind when I think of a book that changed my life. I can't say that this is the one book that changed my life in some irrevocable way, this one book above all others, but I will say that at critical times it's reminded me of just how much can be stuffed into the novel, and how much any one sentence can do.

I honestly can't remember when I first read it. It must have been in my twenties. I think I was about twenty-seven. Growing up in or near Chicago, you live in the shadow of Bellow. I'd read him before, *Dangling Man* and *Seize the Day*, but neither struck me with the hammer blow of *Herzog*.

One page in, sure, *Herzog* is so different from just about anything that preceded it that you know you're in the presence of something extraordinary. Then, when you hit this passage, you know you're listening to a singular voice:

And why? Because he let the entire world press upon him. For instance? Well, for instance, what it means to be a man. In a city. In a century. In transition. In a mass. Transformed by science. Under organized power. Subject to tremendous controls. In a condition caused by mechanization. After the late failure of radical hopes. In a society that was no community and devalued the person. Owing to the multiplied power of numbers which made the self negligible. Which spent military billions on foreign enemies but would not pay for order at home. Which permitted savagery and barbarism in its own great cities. At the same time, the pressure of human millions who have discovered what concerted efforts and thoughts can do. As megatons of water shape organisms on the ocean floor. As tides polish stones. As winds hollow cliffs. The beautiful supermachinery opening a new life for innumerable mankind.

I had an old paperback, so I felt free to mark it up. I never hesitate to mark up books I own. I've been recommending the book for almost twenty years now. But I haven't had much luck in getting anyone to read it all the way through. I can't quite figure that out.

I've read the book cover to cover about six times, and I've dipped into it hundreds of times. Any time I want to be reminded of how much can be done with a sentence, and how much a novelist can do to speak to the consciousness of an age, and do that with phenomenal musicality, I find one of my copies of Herzog.

I collect *Herzog* copies. I have some very funny pulplike paperbacks from the 1970s, and some old hardcovers from the '60s, some very pristine and some very worn-out copies. I keep one, a beat-up paperback with the cover missing, near me when I write.

I don't think it's affected my writing directly, but I do use it as inspiration. Any time a writer is feeling lazy, they should pick up Bellow and be reminded of how much they can or should be doing. On any given page, he puts the whole world and history of Western thought.

Bellow isn't read as much as he should be. There are fervent advocates, but there are plenty more who find him impenetrable or dated. There are some anachronistic ideas in some of his books, but that's to be expected with anyone not of our era, I think. But his work, especially *Herzog*, still sings today.

Dave Eggers is the author of nine books, most recently The Circle *and* A Hologram for the King, *a finalist for the 2012 National Book Award. He founded McSweeney's, an independent publishing company based in San Francisco. Eggers is the cofounder of 826 National and ScholarMatch, a nonprofit organization designed to connect students with resources, schools, and donors to make college possible. He lives in Northern California with his family.*

GILLIAN FLYNN

on *The Westing Game*
by Ellen Raskin

"You never know what's going to happen next"

Once a year, I read Ellen Raskin's *The Westing Game*, because its twisty, weird plot about a pair of sisters and the other occupants of their strange lakeside apartment complex sucked me right in when I read it for the first time as a kid. All of my novels are influenced in some small way by *The Westing Game*, which is technically YA lit, but with a deeply clever mystery at its heart.

It took me a while to really understand how much I loved the mystery, because I was so captivated by the lead character of Turtle Wexler. She was a thirteen-year-old protagonist, but she wasn't a teenager who was pretty, or popular, or a mean girl. She was something entirely different. She's not shy, she's not timid, she's bold and curious and far more interested in defining other people than in being defined by them.

I wanted to be like Turtle Wexler. Gradually, as I followed Turtle and her avid sleuthing, I got sucked in and started to see how clever Raskin was in her plotting. The entire "Westing Game" is an elaborate puzzle filled with wordplay, but with this glorious plan behind it that makes it less whimsical and more diabolical. The plot is that an eccentric millionaire has died and left his fortune to two of his sixteen relatives, organized by him into eight mismatched and often fractous pairs. The pair that uncovers his killer will win both his money and control of his company.

So far, so good, and there is so much that I don't want to spoil for anyone who hasn't read this novel yet. It's a murder mystery wrapped in a word game disguised as a treasure hunt enveloped in a competition. I also learned a lot about life and teamwork from this book. You never know what's going to happen next. Don't rely on your memory—take notes! Everyone has a secret heartache—even grownups. Be willing to work with someone who doesn't seem cool or interesting; a lot goes on behind closed doors.

Although it was supposed to be a YA novel, reading *The Westing Game* felt, to me, like the most adult experience I'd had as a reader up to that point. I've learned a lot about Raskin over the years, including the fact that she started out as an illustrator, which makes sense given the terrific descriptions of the characters. But I think the thing that impresses me most is how she has said she didn't know the outcome until she wrote the final pages. In a sense, reader and writer are figuring things out together, which is why I think there's such a grown-up feel. The author wasn't pedantically planting clues for readers to pick up; she was really following the story line.

I love *The Westing Game* so much that I'd never try to rewrite it, or write my own version, but you can be sure that *Gone Girl* bears its influence. "Amazing" Amy's love of riddles and wordplay would make her a worthy adversary for Turtle.

Speaking of Amy, many readers now know her fate is quite different from what they might have imagined. That's another idea I gleaned from Raskin's plot. Not only do things occur that are bittersweet, but things are mentioned that take place far into the characters' futures.

Unfortunately for all of us, Ellen Raskin's future wasn't a long one. She died in 1984, and I wish we had more of her books to read and love and change us. But I hope that in sharing my well-honed obsession with *The Westing Game* I'll encourage someone else to make it an annual read.

Gillian Flynn is the bestselling author of Sharp Objects, Dark Places, *and* Gone Girl, *the latter a major motion picture starring Ben Affleck. She lives in Chicago with her husband and their two children.*

AMANDA FOREMAN

on *Animal Farm*
by George Orwell

"Words can set you free"

There is no book that has actually changed my life. I'm not convinced that people go through Damascene conversions like that as a kind of general rule. I think what happens is that people are already on a path toward change, and it's gradual, and then the thing they identify as life-changing is that defining moment when that change is crystallized into thoughts and words.

But it's extremely rare that humans actually float from State A to State B in the course of a few hours or overnight because they read something. I think it can happen, and I think certainly there may be religious conversions that happen this way, but personally I'm incredibly skeptical. The majority of those you have spoken to will have shaped that narrative to fit the circumstances that you've asked them to fit into. I'm not saying they're lying. I just don't think humans actually function that way. The real process of human conversion from A to B is much more elongated.

So I cannot say in all honesty that there was a single book that changed my life. Is there a book that helped me to redirect the course of my life? I would say yes. It didn't change me when I read it at the time, but upon reflection, in all subsequent actions, both politically and philosophically in terms of my writing, I would say yes. And that book would be *Animal Farm* by George Orwell.

I was introduced to that because I was a schoolchild. My reaction to it then was specific: I felt the horror when the horse, Boxer, is carted off to the knacker's, betrayed by the pigs. I felt a sort of shock and fear, too, at the end when the animals looked through the window and it was almost impossible to tell the pigs from the men.

And so it's a powerful fable. But it was only once I left school and went to university that I began to see that when people, good people, are subjected to peer pressure, they start to fall in line. When I was at Sarah Lawrence as an undergraduate, we had a sit-in that lasted for almost two months. And the issues that were discussed were important. They were part of a sincere trend by the students to stress what they felt were very important issues, dealing with racism and instructional racism, institutional racism, unfairness, classes, sexism in society as a whole. And what they also felt was manifesting itself in some parts in the college.

But that raised sincere plans, too, that became demagogic, intimidating toward the censors. It shut down debate rather than increased it. Then one night a group of anonymous students went around and they spray-painted around the campus "Four legs good, two legs bad." It was one of those important moments in which you could see somehow it released the campus from its spiral of internal despair and self-anger and often I think kind of misplaced anger which had shut down the very things they had wanted to open up, i.e., dialogue, openness to ideas, willingness to change, embracing all views.

I think those events set me on my own personal path toward kind of having an individual moral compass. What *Animal Farm* really meant to me is the importance of the individual moral compass. I mean that you can be smart and completely out of step with society. But the individualistic message of *Animal Farm* is also about how groups of individuals following moral compasses can result in positive moral collectivism—and certainly moral collectivism has been my own personal guiding light. Everyone knew what those words meant: "Four legs good, two legs bad." It showed us that words can set you free, at least set your mind free.

Thoreau once said, "It's not what you look at that matters, it's what you see." Orwell did that his entire life. All of his books encompass not simply what's in front of you, but a perspective. I think in order to have a view, you need to be able to step back. He had a very strong and clearly articulated moral conscience that was based on clearly defined principles of individualism, fairness, a sense of collective belonging—and built on the foundation of history.

He affects me still. The idea of something changing my life and then ending doesn't make any sense to me. I feel that I'm following in his wake.

Dr. Amanda Foreman wrote A World on Fire, Georgiana, Duchess of Devonshire, *and many other popular books of history. She writes "Historically Speaking" for the* Wall Street Journal *and is working on a documentary about women's history for the BBC.*

MARTIN FROST

on *The Making of the President 1960*
by Theodore White

"It was immediately galvanizing"

I had no notion of becoming a politician when I was a college student at the University of Missouri, so when Theodore White's *The Making of the President* came out in 1961, I may have picked it up just to read for pleasure. However, it was immediately galvanizing; as soon as I'd gotten a few pages into the book, I wanted to be part of the city and system that was involved in "making" a president.

I had had some interest in politics, mostly local and mostly from the sidelines. My grandfather was the mayor of Henderson, Texas, and my great-uncle served in the Texas state senate. The whole family took part in what was essentially small-town politics.

But White's book was fascinating, all about the ins and outs of a presidential campaign. I remember reading the famous section that describes the Kennedy-Nixon television debates, which I had seen the previous year. I decided I wanted to cover politics.

The first exposure I had to the inner workings of a campaign was in 1965, covering the Hill for *Congressional Quarterly*.

Soon after that I made the decision that I'd rather try to influence events instead of report on them, so I went to law school at Georgetown and then returned to Texas—to get involved in what was essentially small-town politics. But White's book had given me a sense of the things you had to do to get from one level to the next, so I was more ready than I once might have been. White made the whole process sound so exciting and interesting and worthwhile. Of course, it wasn't always that way.

But Teddy White helped me get interested in how the game is played, even during its lulls. I started thinking about what might happen if I got elected. What would I want to try to accomplish? It gave me a perspective on what's involved in things from the smallest meeting in a congressional office all the way up to the White House.

Martin Frost served as a representative (D-TX) in Congress for twenty-six years, including four as chair of the House Democratic Caucus. A senior partner at Polsinelli, Frost works on a number of public policy issues and is chairman of the board of advisers for the National Endowment for Democracy.

TAVI GEVINSON

on *Mr. Wilson's Cabinet of Wonders*
by Lawrence Weschler

"That shimmer, the capacity for such delirious confusion"

The book that changed my life is *Mr. Wilson's Cabinet of Wonder* by Lawrence Weschler. I became obsessed with David Wilson's Museum of Jurassic Technology in Los Angeles after visiting it in high school. I've read many of the museum's own publications and have a View-Master with little slides of the exhibits.

It was unlike anything I'd ever seen. I feel like sometimes I try to explain it and have to keep saying, "No, you don't understand," because it's not simply an eclectic collection of found objects. They're elaborate displays of scientific theories, discoveries, and legends. One of my favorites is the room of mosaics made from the scales of butterfly wings, that you have to look at through microscopes. Wilson is thorough. He's created an intricate system for understanding and appreciating life. Weschler's book does an amazing job of expanding on that appreciation, instead of operating merely as biography or journalism. It's a very loving portrait of Wilson, and of the mysteries of existence.

This book recontextualized the way I saw science in relation to art. My work as an editor, the art director of the *Rookie Year-books*, and a writer, is supported by a habit of forming connections across different mediums of art. I love being able to form a constellation of ideas and visual motifs from a variety of sources. But I always thought of myself as creative, not inclined towards math or science. The museum, and Weschler's book, showed me how science is creative, and connected to all of the above. It made my work far more dynamic because I stopped accounting just for manmade art. Wilson talks often about the Greater Chain of Being, and the museum and book opened me up to links I had not seen before. One of the exhibits at the museum is about the seventeenth-century scholar Athanasius Kircher, and it's called "The World is Bound by Secret Knots." I began noticing so many more of the secret knots after reading this book.

I read *Mr. Wilson's Cabinet of Wonder* because my dad had ordered it after we visited the museum. He was so taken with it that he recommended it to me. I wound up interviewing Wilson for *Rookie*, and he gave me beautiful advice about remaining open to the world even through feelings of extreme isolation. I used his words in a keynote address I've now delivered to thousands of people. I also used Weschler's explanation of what makes the Museum so special: "It's that very shimmer, the capacity for such delicious confusion, Wilson sometimes seems to suggest, that may constitute the most blessedly wonderful thing about being human."

Tavi Gevinson is the founder and editor in chief of Rookie *magazine, which is aimed primarily at teenage girls. Gevinson, who became an online sensation at the age of eleven for her blog* Style Rookie, *has since shifted her focus to pop culture and feminism.*

LEV GROSSMAN

on *Waiting for Godot*
by Samuel Beckett

"Look, look, I finally got it!"

My parents were both academics, incredibly austere literary figures. My father was a poet and professor of English at Brandeis,
and later at Johns Hopkins. My mother was a professor at Smith
and Brandeis . . . The point is, they had advanced degrees in literature, they taught literature at fancy universities, and literature
was a big deal in our house. (Most people who had my father as a
professor agree that he is the most terrifying they ever had.)

But I found literature boring. I liked to read fantasy and sci-fi
and comic books. I liked video games, Dungeons and Dragons.
The great books that were so important to my parents made no
impression on me, and I couldn't figure out why.

So, as adolescents do, I naturally assumed that it was because
there was something wrong with me. I felt bad about it, like I was
sort of shut out of this world that my parents were constantly
celebrating. You know those Magic Eye posters you stare at, and

some people can see the object in them instantly, and for others, nothing ever appears? That's what the books my parents loved were like for me.

For some reason, when I was in ninth grade, we went as a family to see Samuel Beckett's *Waiting for Godot*. We weren't a theatergoing family. The production we saw, at the American Repertory Theater in Cambridge, is now legendary.

I was dreading the performance. I had been exposed to culture in many different ways, including classical-music concerts and being dragged through museums. My parents would be in ecstasy on these excursions, and it kind of freaked me out. The only thing that slightly reassured me about this very literary play is that one of the actors had been on *Perfect Strangers*. He'd been on a sitcom. Maybe he'd be a little bit funny?

Waiting for Godot is not like anything else. I felt as though, you know, somebody was saying, "Let's just drop the bullshit for a second. Let's actually talk about what life is, what's really happening here. Let's forget the flowery language and everybody's dignity and let's allow people's pants to fall down." Much, much later I learned that Beckett had grown interested in the theater through vaudeville. He basically took a vaudeville act and made it literary.

Except: it was a vaudeville act about life, and the effect on me was just stunning. I was a moody adolescent who thought the world was a terrible place and I didn't know what I was doing there, because nothing had a point. All the things that people were constantly telling you had a point, didn't. All the things that were meant to make you happy, couldn't.

One of these things I was most aware of as a teenager is how different my life was from the fantasy literature that I read. My life was not exciting. I assumed everyone else's was. Mine was just one bad thing after another. I was physically little. I never won anything.

And then you had these two clowns staggering around the stage eating carrots and talking about death and their pants were falling down and they'd do yoga and they'd fall over. It was just hilarious but it was also true. All this stuff I'd thought just stayed permanently inside you, that words couldn't fit—Beckett had found a way to say it.

One part of me wanted to say to my parents, "Look, look, I finally got it!" I probably did, at the time; I craved their approval so much. But the funny, wonderful thing was that *Waiting for Godot* released me, in a way, from craving that approval. Suddenly, I was in on something. I was in on a great secret. But I wasn't in on it with them; I was in on it with Samuel Beckett.

I'd had the appeal of fantasy down from an early age, but until *Godot*, I didn't understand the appeal of reality. Now all of the fiction I write is about negotiating between the two, and it's all because of that play.

Once, a close friend of my father's, Richard Howard, heard I loved Beckett, whom he translated. He said, "Oh, do you want me to tell him anything when I'm in Paris?" I froze completely and ran to my room and hid there for like an hour. When I finally came out, I said, "I can't think of anything, so yeah, don't tell him anything." At the time I thought that was a real failure on my part. But now? I think Beckett would appreciate the fact that I couldn't find the language to fit my feelings.

Lev Grossman is the author of the Magicians *trilogy and is the book critic for* Time *magazine. He lives in Brooklyn with his wife, two daughters, and one son.*

TIM GUNN

on *Let Us Now Praise Famous Men*
by James Agee

"Works are to be savored, not devoured"

While attending art school in the early 1970s in Washington, DC, a favorite teacher, William Christenberry, introduced me to the collected works of James Agee: author, journalist, poet, screenwriter, and film critic. Although I had previously studied English literature, I had never heard of Agee, so I was naturally curious and eager to experience his work. My introduction was *Let Us Now Praise Famous Men*, a telling of Agee's many weeks living among sharecroppers in Alabama during the Great Depression. The photographer Walker Evans documented the experience, and his photographs accompany the book. But it was Agee's autobiographical novel, *A Death in the Family*, that totally captivated me.

I felt the impact of Agee's work the moment I first encountered his work. It was immediate. It was palpable and only increased with each successive work of his. His work inspired a series of sculptures that I created in 1975–76, and Agee's short story "A Mother's Tale" was the catalyst for eight months of vegetarianism (!).

Agee's works are to be savored, not devoured. I will read and reread single paragraphs before moving on. Agee's command of the written word is exquisite. In *Let Us Now Praise Famous Men*, there is a single page on which only the following appears:

The house had now descended
All over Alabama the lamps are out

For some emotional reason, those words take my breath away, as does the prologue to *A Death in the Family*, which has its own title—"Knoxville: Summer, 1915." That prologue is so rich and lyrical that it inspired the composer Samuel Barber to set excerpts of it to music in a composition created for the soprano Eleanor Steber, but I love the rendition from Leontyne Price (you can find it on iTunes: *Leontyne Price Sings Barber*). Furthermore, the playwright Tad Mosel adapted the book for his play *All the Way Home*. Agee and, later, Mosel each received a Pulitzer Prize for these works.

When it comes to books, I have OCD. I remove the cover of hardbacks to preserve them while reading, and it's all I can do to keep from wearing archival gloves for turning the pages. There are hundreds of books in my apartment, most of which are so well cared for that people can't believe that they have been read. They have!

I reread. Frequently. For me, rereading is spiritual fuel. It's analogous to revisiting works in a museum, which I also do with frequency. With each new reading, I discover more dimensions of meaning and acquire more dimensions of comprehension.

Agee's work has had a profound impact on how I write. While I certainly don't write like Agee, I aspire to achieve the authenticity and integrity of his voice.

Long ago, I gave away to a dear friend my original copy of *Let Us Now Praise Famous Men*. Since then, I've bought and given away at least a dozen copies, all hardback. I now have a paperback edition. I still have my original paperback copy of *A Death in the Family*, which shows signs of lots of love.

I don't know how many people are aware of Agee's powerful and arresting writing. I haven't even mentioned his screenplays, including for the iconic film *The African Queen*, nor have I mentioned his seminal film criticism. His is a timeless voice and it's as relevant today as it was in the first half of the last century.

Tim Gunn is an American fashion and television personality best known for his role on the reality show Project Runway.

CARLA HALL

on *The Giving Tree*
by Shel Silverstein

"It's a special gift to have found a story like that"

Shakespeare, Mother Goose, and original plays from improv exercises were all memorable when I was attending theater camp, but I really loved when we performed a play that was based on the book *The Giving Tree*, by Shel Silverstein. The message of that story felt profound to me as a child, and it still resonates just as strongly (if not even more) now that I am an adult.

It's the tree itself that the character in *The Giving Tree* feels a connection to. I feel that same connection with both the culinary arts and performing arts. Art is something that has given me exactly what I've needed at different points in my life. The last time I grabbed *The Giving Tree* off the shelf was actually fairly recently. I love the simplicity of the message, and I'm always astounded at how every time I read it, I take away a little something more to apply to my life. It's a special gift to have found a story like that, that touches me, and that has actually helped shape me and my outlook to approaching life. It awakens my resolve to truly appreciate life, the journey, and what I have been able to accomplish, and what still remains to be done.

When I look at Silverstein's book, with its line drawings and simple text, I sort of check in and do a report card on myself. Where am I now? What makes me happy? The words stay the same over time, but the meaning changes. I see my life when I reread that book.

Of course, it also refocuses my "giving" side. It reminds me of the pride I have of my community in Washington, DC, and my growing community in NYC. *The Giving Tree* always reminds me that creating and nurturing my community is a very important part of life. Giving and growing go hand in hand. To quote my mother (which she always loves), "I don't care if you go to the grocery store today, or the post office, or the library. Get to know the people who are serving you." I keep that in mind every day. It's the difference between walking up to a counter to ask for help and looking the person helping me in the eye (rather than focusing down on my phone or anything else that might be distracting me at the moment). And in the end, that brings me numerous opportunities to speak with members of my community, and to give a bit of me back in the interaction (even if it is just a friendly smile), and grow as a result of those interactions.

The other day I was on my way to my evening hot yoga class and a conversation I had recently had with someone had me thinking about emotional eating. And this phrase came to me: "You can either eat your emotions or bake your power."

As soon as those words formed, I thought, "*That* is my next mission." Bake your power! Baking is so community oriented. For centuries, bakers have shared starters and equipment and ovens, people have shared ingredients and pans and tins of cookies.

There is power in sharing. Power in giving. Oh, my, this book is still changing my life!

Carla Hall is a cohost of ABC's popular lifestyle series The Chew *and is best known as a competitor on Bravo's* Top Chef. *Her latest cookbook,* Carla's Comfort Food: Favorite Dishes from Around the World, *came out in 2014. She lives and cooks in Washington, DC.*

TONY P. HALL

on the Bible

"This is important"

The number one book that changed my life is the Holy Bible. What I feel is if this is God, we should be studying what He says about life and the way we're supposed to live. He's pretty clear about how we are meant to deal with the issues of poverty and hunger.

There are over twenty-five hundred verses in the Old and New Testaments that deal with these issues. It's the second-most talked-about theme in the Bible, and God is very clear on what He says about it. He does not say that poverty and hunger are good ideas. He says we should take our time and help the poor. He says he wants it solved. That gets my attention, and there are some great Old Testament verses, especially in Proverbs, that say those who care for the poor "lend to me," that is, to God.

He uses the word "lend," meaning "Those people who help the poor honor me." God doesn't say that much in the Bible, and so when He does, I take that very seriously. Not only do you honor God by helping the poor and feeding the hungry; God says he will not forget it. To Him, these are very, very serious and important issues.

I think that God knows mankind and realizes a lot of people are going to look the other way. He knows that the poor don't have much of a voice, especially in politics, especially in DC— look at the lobbyists and other spokespeople. There are no PACs for the poor and hungry. They don't have a lot of clout, and they don't get a lot of attention. They're really voiceless. God knew this, and through the Bible He is saying, "I want you to care. This is important. I want you to be involved."

When I came to Congress, for the longest time I was very in-volved with ambition and success and trying to make something out of myself. When I finally got to the Congress I was mar-ried with children and had money in my pocket. "Boy, I've really arrived, I'm successful." But something happened. I reluctantly attended a prayer breakfast back home in Dayton, Ohio, and I received a message about what God wants us to accomplish that started me on my life's work.

I read, and studied, and prayed, and I became the chairman of a subcommittee on international hunger. In 1984 I traveled to Ethio-pia and I saw twenty-five children die in one morning from hunger. I was walking among masses of people looking for food, medicine, water, help, some who were so exhausted they just lay down and died.

I was lost. I was stunned. As I flew home I thought of all the verses I'd read on those pages in my Bible. I thought, "We do a lot of things in Congress that don't amount to much, but maybe if I concentrate on the issue of feeding the hungry, that will amount to something."

Tony P. Hall was a representative (D-OH) in Congress for twenty years before serving as United States ambassador to the United Na-tions Agencies for Food and Agriculture. He serves as director of the Alliance to End Hunger.

JACOB HEMPHILL

on *The Little Prince*
by Antoine de Saint-Exupéry

"This feeling of peace"

My parents read to me all the time. But my dad was the one who read to me every night before bed, and he started me off with *The Lord of the Rings*. I would sit there and draw pictures while he read to me. Each one of those books is so long, and he read all of them, the trilogy and *The Hobbit*, too. I was only five or six, but I loved them; I never wanted them to end.

I thought I wanted to be a cartoonist, because I would draw all the time, but a funny thing happened on our trips in the family van. I would start saying these little rhymes, like "There's birds in the sky / I can see them with my eye," silly stuff, but I kept doing it.

When I was six or seven we moved to Africa for a couple of years. From my earliest memory I have always had this image of a round hill with a little square house on it and a tree next to it. Whenever I would think of that house and hill and tree I would get this feeling of peace, and I was always trying to get back to that vision, especially if I was angry or had a nightmare. One day we went to a bookstore and there was a book with "my picture" on its cover, *The Little Prince*.

I loved everything about that book and that story. Reading it made me feel like you could be a kid who felt like an adult, and a kid who saw adults as children. You could meet someone who had a profound effect on you, and by telling them your story, you could have a profound effect on them. But the Little Prince's rose really blew my mind. Everywhere he goes, he just wants to get back to his little rose; to everyone else, it looks like every single other rose. Why is it so important?

I've read *The Little Prince* so many times in the almost three decades since I discovered it, and I think I finally know why that rose is so important. It's one thing to love something. It's another thing to care for it, to nurture it and to keep it alive and growing. That idea inspired a song on our new record, called "Lightning": "I was never really good at flowers, 'cause there's many and they all smell good / I was never really good at heaven, making promises like I always could / But you came and struck me like —lightning / That is the heavenly flower . . ."

A musician writes a song about a story in a book, and the feeling that story gives him is there because of his father, and his father is there because of love. Yes, artists connect everything like it's one big thing. I thought I was going to be a cartoonist until my father gave me a guitar when I was thirteen. The first music I really loved was bluegrass, which is a way of passing stories down to generations just like stories and books. After bluegrass, I got into reggae and Bob Marley, and I realized Marley was passing a story along to the entire world, a story about life as a big circle.

Jacob Hemphill is the lead guitarist and vocalist for Soja, a Grammy-nominated reggae band with a new album titled Amid the Noise and Haste.

JUAN FELIPE HERRERA

on the poetry of Federico García Lorca

"Different things that magnetize us"

In the late 1960s and early 1970s I used to stroll around San Francisco's Mission District, and at Twenty-Third Street there was a bookstore, the Libreria Nacional, that sold books in Spanish. It was the only store that sold books in Spanish. It was there that I found a beautiful burgundy leather edition of The Complete Works of Federico García Lorca, hundreds and hundreds of onionskin pages with his plays and his poems and his ink drawings, too.

I grew up as a library and bookstore stroller. I lived in downtowns, and they were my entertainment, my television, my everything. Walking down the street, I might learn about Jerry Lewis, Elizabeth Taylor, *National Geographic*, kooky things, beautiful things, astonishing things, even horrific things—it was from *National Geographic* that I learned about the Holocaust and I'm glad I did.

There was Hare Krishna, Lead Belly, the Beatles, and somehow somewhere in there someone talked to me about Lorca. I
hadn't read much of his work but he was one amazing psychedelic
poet. He wrote in the vernacular of Andalucia and his dreamy
quality was mesmerizing to me. It was also extremely real. For
instance, when I got to "Lament for Ignacio Sánchez Mejías,"
his long poem about the bullfighter, I read it and was struck by
the repetition he used of various dramatic moments happening
at five o'clock in the afternoon, because I happened to have seen
the documentary about Mejias as part of a double feature. A documentary about a bullfighter gored to death—and *Bambi*. Can
you imagine? My grandmother and I watched both films while
eating lemon meringue pie with our hands in the back row of the
theater. While death was on the screen we scooped lemon paste
out of an aluminum pie plate with our hands.

When I found the Lorca book I was around twenty-one, just
a complete dreamer and wanderer who loved art and painters and
philosophers and poets and music; I wasn't much encumbered by
the idea of vocation and career. I was just busy loving books and
art, whatever I could get my hands on. Bold hypnotic writers and
artists moved me before the work began for me.

It was the times, it was my temperament, but it was also my
upbringing. We had very little: rice and beans and salsas and
Roman Meal wheat bread, sometimes a little spinach. But if we
had very little materially, we also had very little to be worried
about. I had a little apartment by this time and I was living in a
kind of radical happiness. I was at UCLA and after my classes
were done I had the rest of the day to wander around. I had
already been reading a lot of German literature in translation,
and I loved the extremes of Hesse and Wolf and Nietzsche and
Schopenhauer and their language took me into a dreamland, so

when I discovered Lorca I was already on his plane and I wanted to write like that.

I kind of followed his style. I was reading and looking, Cocteau, Picasso, Man Ray. I wrote little fantasy theater works and made attempts I thought were similar to Lorca's. In a way it was all very American, part of our smorgasbord. Sometimes we're in another country and we see that people think the magnet is the United States—but here in the United States we have a different kind of palette, different things that magnetize us.

Lorca is always with me now. He's not going to tell you what's going on. He's going to begin with pure magic, the broken guitar and the red table. There's your beginning. I used to read him out loud before a mirror, and I would orchestrate these readings as if I had an invisible choir I could direct. I would read the lines out loud and then move my right hand around as I was reciting, directing . . .

Juan Felipe Herrera was recently named the twenty-first poet laureate of the United States. He is the father of five children and lives with his partner, fellow poet Margarita Robles, in Fresno, California.

DAN HESSE

on *The Republic*
by Plato

"It made me think about how to live"

I'm an avid reader—but not always of books. I read things on the Internet, my *Wall Street Journal*, white papers, business journals. A lot of the books that have really affected my life have been business books, because that's what I do, that's my worldview. I want to know more about people who have been successful in business, how business is changing, and how it helps or hinders the world.

But the book that probably changed my life most fundamentally was one I read in college, and that was Plato's *Republic*. It was my sophomore or junior year at Notre Dame, in a philosophy of politics course. Notre Dame is, of course, a Catholic university and the religious angle permeates just about every aspect of life there. I know things have changed a lot, but the Roman Catholic idea of heaven and afterlife is still very important to the school.

To read Plato and learn about human beings who did not

have this idea was revolutionary for me. I'd been brought up very strictly and had never heard about anyone who didn't believe in the Christian concept of heaven. Yet here were these ancient Greek men, Plato and his teacher Socrates, with their own religious faith—"The gods are watching"—but a completely different idea of why men should be good. I'd always been taught that you have to be good in order to make it into heaven. I'd never thought before that being a good person might be something you should consider because, as Socrates taught, it is the good person who should be leading other people. Being good meant acknowledging truth as far as you possibly could, and that was what led to greatness.

It made me think about how to live, a way to live that had nothing to do with religion. Socrates shows Plato how to argue, to make a logical argument for being good. Socratic dialogue was a way to use logic, and it was a way to use logic so that while you were questioning others, you were learning how they thought, learning what drove them, so that ultimately, if you wanted to, you could persuade them around to your point of view.

A little more of my own history: The way I stood out, when I began in business, was in sales. I cut my teeth as a salesperson, because selling isn't talking, contrary to what most people believe—it's listening. You have to listen to your potential customer and find out what they value and what would satisfy them. If you do that, you can then construct a pitch that pulls all of that in and closes the sale.

So logic and listening are very important in sales, but the reason they're crucial to my career success is because when you become a manager, you have to listen to your employees. They are your customers now, because without them, you're not going to be selling anything at all.

I still have my original paperback copy of Plato's *Republic*, beat-up and crusty and covered in highlighter, and I do go back to it from time to time, mostly to the parts that have the most highlighted lines, since I know that those were lines important to me. Here I am, telling you about a book that's the very height of agnostic thought. I'm still a practicing Catholic. I attend weekly mass. I'm very involved in the University of Notre Dame, and my son is now a student there. But two men who believed in a completely different spiritual system than I do, two men who lived thousands of years ago, passed on lessons that are for and of this world, and they changed my life.

Dan Hesse was the CEO of Sprint until 2014. He lives in Kansas City, Missouri.

CARL HIAASEN

on *Car*
by Harry Crews

"Boundaries are wonderfully flexible"

When I was eighteen or nineteen, a book came out that changed my life because it fueled my own ambition to tell twisted stories that might someday come true.

Being a Floridian, I gravitated to any new fiction that was set in the state. I'd already raced through everything by John D. MacDonald, when along comes *Car* by Harry Crews. I was still in school, but I had an eye on wanting to be a writer. The plot of *Car* was fantastically subversive—a Jacksonville car dealership dreams up a promotion scheme where a guy eats a Ford Maverick from bumper to bumper. They use a blowtorch or something to cut it up into bite-sized pieces.

The whole concept was so warped, I loved every word of it. This was in the time of Vonnegut, too. Both he and Crews helped me see that basically anything's possible when you sit down to write. Anything.

When you're young you think, "What boundaries can I push? How much can I get away with? What will people read? What will they actually buy?"

In the early 1970s, you might have thought, "Who would read a book about a guy eating a car?" But my world, my Florida, even in those days was getting chaotic and bizarre. The madness was just hatching, and Crews was one of the first to put it on display. I don't know how well *Car* sold, but it got great reviews.

For a writer the lesson was clear: Boundaries are wonderfully flexible, and the envelope cannot only be pushed—it can be exploded. *Car* was funny as hell, but also dark. Its not-so-absurd premise was that, as a country, we were unspooling in the wrong direction. This was 1972, remember. Vietnam, Nixon. And the auto dealer saying, "We're just trying to sell some cars." With a man swallowing a ton of steel, one cube at a time!

Crews was Florida's Hunter S. Thompson, eccentric and volatile. His writing class at the University of Florida was so popular that I couldn't get in. My brother Rob did, and within two weeks, Crews challenged him to a fistfight. He didn't like the way my brother had interpreted a novel the class was studying. By then, I already knew I wanted to write about Florida and its bizarre place in the American dream. What Crews showed me, and other writers, was that we could pull it off.

At this point the dial on weird behavior in Florida is way past ten. With eighteen million people living here, the smorgasbord of outrageous true-life material is rich and vast. And these pilgrims keep coming, no matter what.

Of course, writing my column for the *Miami Herald* always gives a jolt of inspiration for the novels. It's not just the daily sleaze and corruption, but the fountain of strange, true stories. The stuff would be impossible to make up, and I poach shamelessly while

I'm working on plots and scenes for the books.

When you write humor, you want people to be laughing for the right reasons, for the human foolishness and absurdity, and not just for the slapstick. There seems to be a Florida connection to practically every major national news story, from Watergate to Bush-Gore, from 9/11 to Donald Trump. For a satirist, this place is heaven. Characters that inhabit our fiction can't help but offer social commentary.

Yet, as Harry Crews knew, Florida isn't just an amusement park for the depraved. It's always been a destination for outlaws and naive dreamers, a place of tropic allure and mystery. And even now that much of it has been paved and stampeded, it's still—mysteriously, to me—attracting people. They get here and they're surprised. *Oh my God! It's crowded! It's expensive! Look at this crime!*

And among these thousands of newcomers every day are the vulnerable—elderly retirees, immigrants eager for work, poor families looking for a fresh start—trailed inevitably by con men and predators. Why? Because they're dreamers, too. Bad dreamers, yes. But they're coming here for the same reason: to make a life in the sunshine.

Carl Hiaasen has been writing about Florida since his father gave him a typewriter at age six. Hiaasen writes a Sunday column for the Miami Herald, *and is the author of many bestselling novels, including* Bad Monkey *and* Skinny Dip.

TOMMY HILFIGER

on *Steve Jobs*
by Walter Isaacson

"It's a learning experience"

I like to read books about successful individuals. How these people think, what makes them think, is something I find very inspiring. For many years I've been attracted to what's successful, to what makes people successful, and how these people turn failures into successes.

One book that really affected me was *Steve Jobs* by Walter Isaacson, because it shows that everyone, even a brilliant maverick like Jobs, makes a lot of mistakes along the way. Somehow, in that book, Isaacson shows that Jobs realized there's a benefit to making these mistakes. It's a learning experience. You look at the benefit side, and you realize that mistakes are almost gifts.

In any situation you have a lot of setbacks, and if you let them get to you, you are not going to be successful. You have to look at them as a challenge. Look, there's another obstacle—how do I get around this one? The Jobs story shows that there were a lot of starts and stops in his career, and a lot of situations that could have influenced him to give it up at any certain time. But he was so passionate about what he was doing, he kept going. That's a tribute to him, and a form of genius in itself.

I'm dyslexic, so I've always had difficulty in reading. I'm not one to indulge in a heavy novel or complicated philosophical book, and I save my reading energy for books that truly inspire me. JFK's *Profiles in Courage*, Obama's *Dreams from My Father*, Martin Luther King Jr.'s works. Dr. King was an iconic bridge builder who unlocked freedom for a lot of people. These people have major, major motivation and a desire to do something. There is also something unusual in how they think, I almost always find when I read their books or books about them.

Although it's never been easy for me to read, I do find it convenient. You basically carry a book and read it at will, which is fantastic for people like me who travel a great deal. I still read a lot of paper books, not because I don't think e-reading is fantastic—I do—but because I don't have to worry about plugging anything in or losing power and all that kind of thing when I have a paper book with me.

Tommy Hilfiger is an internationally famous designer and CEO of the Tommy Hilfiger Group, which offers a wide range of American-inspired apparel and accessories.

ERIC IDLE

on Life-Changing Books

"Books get better with age"

Life-changing books?

I'm not sure that happened for me.

One learned to love books as one learned to love women: Gradually. And then with mounting passion. And then with more expertise, and discernment. And finally, with more love.

Life-changing books?

I seriously doubt it happens as you suggest, that somewhere in an old corner of a dusty locker there is a fading, well-thumbed copy, of what, exactly? *Bleak House?* Of course I *would* say that now but it's not true. I was slow to love Dickens. We had to read *Great Expectations* for exams. I didn't love Dickens at first, not until he became a compulsory paper at Cambridge, when a whole exam, one of five, was purely on Dickens, and I read *Our Mutual Friend* with mounting pleasure in the Dordogne.

So I am going to eschew your neat mathematical formula and tell you the complex truth.

We were taught to read and love books. It isn't like a love of football which strikes you suddenly. It creeps up on you. It removes you from the boredom of a boarding school into the subtleties of another world. It still is my favorite escape. I am never without a book.

Early reading loves? Sure. *The Alexandria Quartet* by Lawrence Durrell. Does anyone still read those? I remember at sixteen devouring *Dr. Zhivago* in the sand dunes in Cornwall, wondering why older men in mackintoshes slyly eyed my innocent self. The poetry I read in adolescence, T. S. Eliot—"The Waste Land," "The Love Song of J. Alfred Prufrock"—inspired a torrent of bad verse.

At eighteen I began to really enjoy D. H. Lawrence: *Sons and Lovers. Lady Chatterley's Lover*. And Gerard Manley Hopkins, the weird Jesuit priest: "I caught this morning morning's minion." Or "Margaret art thou grieving / Over Goldengrove unleaving?"

The fact is, books get better with age. As you learn to become a better reader.

I now reread Jane Austen with more joy. Dickens with pure joy. *The Great Gatsby* is my favorite reread. How do you get more out of a book each time? That's the miracle. Answers on a plain essay booklet, please . . . Nabakov is still the best writer ever to have written about reading. *Lectures on Literature*. A glimpse into the craft of the thing from a working writer's perspective.

So now I read omnivorously. I devour books. I don't read newspapers or magazines, or watch TV. On a long flight I ignore the battery of multichanneled bullshit for a good book.

I have kept a reading diary since 1993. And I now share it online. See www.ericidle.com/reading/ for what I have been reading since 2009.

So no, I'm sorry. My life is not changed by a single book. My life is changed by books. On a daily basis.

Eric Idle is an English comedian, actor, author, singer-songwriter, musician, writer, and comedic composer. Idle is a member of the English surreal comedy group Monty Python, a member of the Rutles, and the author of the Broadway musical Spamalot.

MIRA JACOB

on *The God of Small Things*
by Arundhati Roy

*"Oh, there's a me . . . who's important
enough to have a story?"*

I grew up in the New Mexican desert with very few Indians and ever fewer Syrian Christians. Because I didn't know many other people from our specific community, I thought that my parents' mannerisms were unique to them. All of the literature from South Asia that informed the West was from other groups—Bengalis, Hindus, Northern Indians—and honestly, I didn't recognize their ways. They sure weren't ours. And it did a funny thing to me, not seeing anyone like us anywhere—it made me feel like we didn't really exist.

Then *The God of Small Things* by Arundhati Roy came out. As far as I know, it was the first major literary work about the Syrian Christian community in India. It was definitely the first one to make its way to me in New Mexico. The impact was immediate and huge. It was us, right there, on the page. Well, not really, but the mannerisms, the curses, the odd frictions—they were ours. I thought, wait, there's really a me? A me who's important enough to have a story? It gave me a kind of solidity I didn't have before. It also made me want to do the same thing for other Indian Americans.

The book impacted my actual writing process tremendously because until then, I had assumed that fiction needed to be about things as distant from a writer's reality as possible, that anything else was some shameful cross between cheating, stealing, and lying. But because Roy is a very distant cousin of mine, I knew enough about the family in her book to shake out what was fact and what was fiction. From that, I could map out how and where she had fictionalized portions of a very real experience to get to a certain emotional truth. And I understood fiction as a different thing then—one that used imagination as a chisel against the things that haunt us the most. It was so freeing.

Mira Jacob is the founder of Pete's Reading Series in New York City and has an MFA from the New School for Social Research. She lives in Brooklyn with her husband and son. Her first novel, The Sleepwalker's Guide to Dancing, *was published in 2014.*

BEVERLY JOHNSON

on *John Adams*
by David McCullough

"You learn something totally new"

My father was a steel laborer, but when he was in the army he traveled through Europe and learned a lot of different languages; he also became a lifelong voracious reader, and all of us kids always were, too. I read so much it's crazy, and I wish I were at home right now because I could look at my books and go through them, but I'm in a hotel room in Chicago and I can't. I hate being without them. Even though I try to keep only the books I can't live without, I must have several thousand.

I particularly love to read books about history and books about women—and books about women in history? Bring them on! When I start reading about a woman like Cleopatra or Catherine the Great, I have to read everything I can get my hands on that has to do with them. I really love reading about women who ruled empires, Margaret Thatcher and Eleanor Roosevelt and Queen Elizabeth, and so on.

But one of the books that recently changed my life was David McCullough's biography of John Adams. Adams, unlike Roosevelt, isn't someone whose story we know well. He arrived in history at a pivotal moment, and he threw his intellect and his passion where they needed to go to get things done. McCullough's writing makes you feel just like you were there, and that's important so that you get a sense of how important John Adams was to our young nation.

Adams also got something so important: there's no such thing as retirement. When you have brainpower, that's your gift to the world, and if you don't use it? You lose it. I'm at a really great time in my life. I tried being semiretired, and I got my handicap way down in golf, but I'm an entrepreneur. I want to keep using my brain and stay on the self-discovery road. I read self-help, I read golf books by that hack Nicklaus, I read books about modeling and beauty, and I'm the kind of person who will go back and read the classics, like a Hemingway or a Steinbeck.

Every time, or decade, that you reread a great book, you learn something totally new from it. When I was younger, I didn't understand what the hoopla was about James Baldwin, but when I read him now, I'm just blown away by his prolificacy and courage. I have such respect for writers; it's such a discipline and a gift. It's like singing, I think: you've got it, or you don't.

Beverly Johnson is an actor, producer, and business owner whose memoir, The Face That Changed It All, *was published in 2015 and details her career as the first African American model to appear on the cover of* Vogue *magazine.*

PIPER KERMAN

on *Alice's Adventures in Wonderland*
by Lewis Carroll

"A story that is important enough to tell"

One of the true formative books of my life is *Alice's Adventures in Wonderland* by Lewis Carroll. I put *Alice* on my booklist when I was in prison, as well as *Harriet the Spy* by Louise Fitzhugh. They're both obviously strong female protagonists who are not defined by their relationships to men or boys or romance at all.

That was important to me, too, when I started teaching writing in two state prisons in Ohio. I have a class of men and a class of women; they're separated by gender. All of the students have to have their GED, but otherwise, there's a big range in their interests, intellect, and motivation. What's so striking to me is that within that big range, all of the women have struggled so much more than the men have with thinking about themselves as protagonists, in thinking about their stories in epic terms. We work really hard on the fundamentals of narrative structure in these classes, and the men just took to it. It just doesn't take too much to get men to understand the hero's journey.

Even when we got them to start telling their stories from that perspective, it was much more challenging to get them to think about their lives in epic terms. I thought about Alice and Harriet a lot when I thought about my own perspective on the world and the time I spent in prison thinking about my life.

Alice and Harriet, for example, are allowed to take the central role. If a person in a story doesn't have a really strong sense of agency, then we just don't care. For instance, you might not be interested in a book about a group of women in prison, but when it becomes a book from one woman's perspective, like my book, and that woman talks about her individual journey and struggle, you become invested. It's not because I'm better or more important than the other women; it's just a human thing, a way we focus best.

So yes, women are much more relational, in and out of prison. Women are thinking about relationships a lot more as they are experiencing the world and as they write.

But I want my students to think about how important each of their lives is. Is your life an epic? A lot of them have heard for a long time that they're not important. Reading books with strong female protagonists, even if those books are about younger female protagonists, can help them reconnect with a sense that they have a story, and a story that is important enough to tell, and to narrate individually.

One of the things I learned during my time in prison through other books—I read a lot—is that what happened to me and what happens to a lot of women who wind up in prisons isn't just about our own stupid choices, but also about our government's drug policy. It's very empowering to understand the context around your incarceration. Knowledge is power, and that power can be used for good. We are only able to do something for others when it's been taught to us. I hope that when people look back to 2010, they will see this decade as a watershed in the way we think about our prison populations and make significant changes in thinking about them and making sure that issues of racial justice and equity are considered equally important as budgets to our penal system.

Piper Kerman wrote the memoir Orange Is the New Black, *which has been adapted by Jenji Kohan into an Emmy– and Peabody Award–winning original series for Netflix. She works with Spitfire Strategies as a communications consultant with nonprofits, philanthropies, and other organizations working in the public interest.*

POROCHISTA
KHAKPOUR

on *Good Morning, Midnight*
by Jean Rhys

"The book was so powerful for me"

Jean Rhys's *Good Morning, Midnight* changed my life, in a not entirely positive way. I first read it in 2005 and plowed through it feverishly. It was so intense, so dark, and seemed to mirror so much of what was wrong with my life, that I sort of felt like it brought on a nervous breakdown that I didn't entirely recover from for years.

I realized as soon as I began the book that it was going to affect me and alter me. The sort of manic impressionism in Rhys's prose echoed the sounds in my head. The book's style was just as intimate to me as the substance, which mirrored my state at that point: a sense of constant uprootedness, incessant yearning and longing for things I couldn't identify, a cycling of bad decisions over and over, an ambiance of unwavering agitated depression, and a sort of loyalty to patterns that were destroying me.

I began the novel very slowly, but as I identified with it more and more, I remember it went very fast, and I could not stop reading it. I vaguely remember canceling some plans to be alone with it, and yet being shocked when it was over so fast.

I have never reread it in whole. I sort of refuse to do that. I'm scared of it. At times, I've hidden it from my reach. I have a sort of superstitious feeling about it, like that it could bring on another breakdown. I know that's silly, but the book was so powerful for me, I fear it.

I'm not sure that it's directly affected my work but it has affected how I see myself as a writer. Perhaps I think there is some of Rhys's own story in this and so for me it hits me hard as a portrait of a young female writer alone. It terrifies me that I am anything like the protagonist, and yet I am somehow grateful to know someone else has lived that way. Perhaps lived to tell it, which seems a miracle.

I just lent it to a gentleman friend this winter, but I think I will be asking for it back soon. I am still close to him, but that book, and that very copy, is such a part of me that even though I'm a bit scared by its presence I'm also scared by its absence.

I think a lot of writers love it—especially women writers, though I recall Tao Lin being a fan and mentioning it on his old blog *Reader of Depressing Books*, where I may have encountered it originally.

I'm sure most people answering your questions talk about books that change their lives in positive ways, books that make them want to write better, books that show them new wisdom, that kind of thing. I think more people should write about the books that disturb them and unnerve them and won't let them sleep at night.

Porochista Khakpour is an Iranian-American novelist, essayist, and writer. Her novels Sons and Other Flammable Objects *and* The Last Illusion *have received much critical acclaim.*

ARLEIGH KINCHELOE

on *Pride and Prejudice*
by Jane Austen

"It transported me"

Last year on tour we were waiting in some municipal office building. They had a couple of shelves of books, you know, the "take one, leave one" kind, like a book exchange. I'd kind of been having a rough time on the road, hadn't gotten my groove on this particular leg of the tour, and I decided to look for something to read, something to take me out of my own head.

There was a copy of *Pride and Prejudice*, and I thought, "I've never read any Jane Austen, and this is as good a time as any." By page twenty-five or thirty I was completely enthralled. The book took me completely out of my everyday thing, which is just what I needed.

It didn't just take me out—it transported me. I think that's why Austen is so good. She's a master of dialogue. After I rampaged my way through the book, I thought, "Nothing really happened!" Nothing happened, except people talking to one another, and she makes that everything. She really figured out human interaction, how it has no era and is really the same across all time. The issues she deals with are so current: love and destiny and jealousy and comfort and a lot more. As much of a time piece as the novel is, you could set it in our own century and it would still work. What a brilliant mind Jane Austen has that she was able to see that, and to paint such a vivid picture of her own time.

My dad's a teacher and I remember calling him and saying, "Dude, why didn't you turn me on to Jane Austen years ago?" He himself had forgotten how amazing her work is, and he reread it, too, and that is now his favorite. I want to say to everyone who reads *Pride and Prejudice* to hold on to how good that book is in your mind.

Now that it's been a year, I might go ahead and pick up another Austen novel. I go through phases with reading; sometimes I find it a little hard. Life is often hard and dark and intense itself, and when I read *The Goldfinch* by Donna Tartt I knew it was really good, but I also found it kind of crushing. The tone of the book has a lot to do with how quickly I can get through it; sometimes I go months and months without reading, getting mentally cleansed. But then again, sometimes I go through pages and pages of reading, which is a great outlet, being who I am, being the only girl on the road for weeks and months at a time. Right now I'm revisiting *Even Cowgirls Get the Blues* by Tom Robbins.

Arleigh Kincheloe is the lead singer of Sister Sparrow and the Dirty Birds, a seven-piece Brooklyn soul band in which her brother, Jackson Kincheloe, plays harmonica. Their latest album, The Weather Below, *was released in 2015.*

LILY KING

on *It's Not the End of the World*
by Judy Blume

"The claustrophobia of family"

The book that changed my life was *It's Not the End of the World* by Judy Blume. I had already loved *Are You There God? It's Me, Margaret*, and it was natural that I would want to read Blume's next novel. But there was a much bigger reason that this one changed me. It helped me process my parents' divorce.

No one else I knew had parents who were getting divorced. It was 1973, and my parents split for good in the summer of 1974. I know that I read *It's Not the End of the World* in hardcover, as I read all of Blume's books, because my mother would buy them for me.

Even though the circumstances were very different between my parents and Karen's in the novel, reading her story made me feel that I had a friend going through this, experiencing her family coming to an end. I read that novel many times—and I'm sure my mother was aware of what she was trying to do in giving it to me.

But aside from the narrator and her voice, from the moment I read Blume, she spoke to me in a way no writer had before. When I was growing up, there were a lot of talking animals in children's literature, and a lot of science fiction for slightly older kids. There was nobody just telling us family tales. So when I stumbled on Judy Blume, I not only felt like "I love this kind of writing, I love this kind of book," but I felt for the first time "I want to do this. I want to write these kinds of things." And I'd never had that before. I really, really credit Judy Blume for that.

Blume was willing to speak to and through young people's minds. I felt like she was at my level, but at the same time guiding me, really helping me be aware not to think just about the pain of my parents breaking up, but through to the larger picture. It's such an interesting and powerful combination: I felt like I needed that book, but I also got so much pleasure out of that book. There are great characters, like the friend the protagonist makes in her father's new "bachelor" apartment building. This new friend is much more sophisticated and cultured; she reads the *New York Times*.

I grew up in Manchester, Massachusetts, and a lot of the books I found in the library were set in the country, on farms. Judy Blume is mainly suburban, but you get a little hit, from things like that girl reading the *Times*, of something bigger and more metropolitan.

For a while, I did want to write for the young adult audience; I felt that I would grow up authoring for children. But, of course, other books came along that shifted my ideas and made me more interested in writing for adults. Finally, I realized that what Judy Blume had taught me is that writing about family, writing about psychological dramas, writing about people in a household—that's vital stuff. I think I've always been interested in the claustrophobia of family.

At first I thought *Euphoria* such a departure for me, because it wasn't about that. But then I went back to what had originally drawn me to the story of Margaret Mead and her husband and lover, which was a scene in a biography of Mead where all three of them are living together in a little hut, and it's such a pressure-cooker situation. I wanted to write about a domestic group under pressure. Here I am, back to 1973, thinking about a domestic group that is splintering. Anyone who has ever said the phrase "just YA literature" does not understand that a book can change your life and keep resonating in your life for decades.

Lily King's novels include The Pleasing Hour, The English Teacher, *and* Father of the Rain. *Her most recent,* Euphoria, *has won numerous awards and was named one of the ten best books of 2014 by the* New York Times Book Review, *is being translated into numerous languages, and will be a feature film.*

JACK KINGSTON

on *How I Raised Myself from Failure
to Success in Selling*
by Frank Bettger

"You know where you stand"

When I was twenty-four years old and just starting my career in properties and casualty insurance, I read *How I Raised Myself from Failure to Success in Selling* by Frank Bettger. I'd been having a difficult time and I was looking for something that would help me out in my career. I didn't think it would be this book; I remember in the old copy I had that the men were still wearing hats and taking trains to work every day. It seemed pretty old-fashioned.

But, believe it or not, the lessons were completely contemporary—or maybe, I should say, the lessons haven't changed. I was a 100 percent commission insurance salesman. I had to learn that it was a numbers game, that I had to make the calls and make the sales. Bettger himself had been in the same position. One of the lines, I remember, that really killed me was "Get a haberdasher." There weren't a lot of those around in 1979!

But I had a friend who worked in fashion for *GQ* who said, "I'm going to be your dress chairman." This was a beer-drinking buddy of mine who just went through my closet and told me what to get rid of. He's now done that three times for me in various stages of my career, and you know what? Bettger was right. It's not so much about spending a lot of money on clothes or being overly concerned with style—it's just that if you're in the public, you've got to dress and look nice. Bettger knew that if something doesn't come naturally to you, you should seek out an expert.

A lot of the advice in the book is about record keeping. Keep track of your numbers, and you're going to have a good year, because you know where you stand. No one likes to be rejected, but sales and politics and many other fields are full of rejection. This book showed me that rejection was part of the game, too.

I've read this book three times now, including this past February as I started my third career as principal at Squire Patton Boggs. I'm a "rainmaker," but it's been a long drought, and the crazy thing is that even though I left one side of the street for the other, within a week people don't return your calls. I found comfort in going back to Bettger and the 1940s truth that it's still the same whether you're working with typewriters and dial-up telephones or tablets and smart devices.

This book is as good as they get, and my son is now a salesperson for Northwestern Mutual, so I've given it to him, too. Speaking of children, one of the best things Bettger recommends is setting up a schedule—and not changing it. Not changing it one bit, ever. I can tell you that in Congress people can and will absorb every minute of your day, and you absolutely never run out of work, so you have to put in the family stuff first and build the rest of your schedule around that. I'm not trying to build myself up as father of the year, but if you don't do that, if you don't put the family in as number one, you'll never get to a baseball game.

Jack Kingston served as a representative (R-GA) in Congress from 1993 to 2015. Now a principal for business development at Squire Patton Boggs, he maintains residences in Savannah and Tybee Island, Georgia.

JEFF KINNEY

on *Inside the Box*
by Drew Boyd and Jacob Goldenberg

"Simple is best"

I've just opened a bookstore. Thank goodness I'd already read *Inside the Box: A Proven System of Creativity for Breakthrough Results* by Drew Boyd and Jacob Goldenberg.

We've all heard plenty about thinking outside the box in the past few years, a phrase that's supposed to mean all kinds of good stuff for creativity—throwing away convention, not being defined by outdated ideas, coming up with as many big, wild things as possible, right?

But a few things have changed my view on outside-of-the-box thinking. The most obvious is that my *Wimpy Kid* books aren't about anything big and wild. They're about simple and safe—at least on the surface. Line drawings, diary entries, growing pains. These are things everyone can understand.

Second, I have a family, and we wanted to figure out how to have the best life together we possibly could. We wanted to live in a place that made sense for work, for extended family, and for stability. My wife and I looked at a map together and decided that Plainville, Massachusetts, would be the town where we could best balance all of those things with each other and for our two boys.

Third, as we've settled into our community, I realized that I didn't want to just live in it—I wanted to contribute to it. A few years ago, I bought a building and thought and thought about what to do with it until I remembered that simple is best. Everyone loves bookstores. Why not open a bookstore?

An Unlikely Story opened in July 2015. Two years ago, I read *Inside the Box*. It changed my thoughts about how to solve problems. It changed my thoughts about how to innovate and create. The thing that's really important about this book and the method its authors suggest is that it's not based on grandstanding, just turning something upside down. It's based on engineering theory and practice, from a man named Genrich Altshuller.

Altshuller and his colleagues learned by studying successful products, really successful products, that there's a pattern to their development, and that pattern can be templated. What are these templates? Really, just five. Subtraction, division, multiplication, task unification, and attribute dependency.

I'll explain, as quickly as possible. Say you have a device, a phone or a tablet. How do you make it better? You could subtract something superfluous—make it thinner. You could divide up tasks—apps. You could multiply its uses—add a keyboard. You could unify its tasks—it's a phone and a camera. You could make one of its attributes depend on something—use GPS services to help friends find you at a café.

Another easy way to think of these templates is through the currently buzzy word "lifehacks." When you think of a new way to do an existing task, a new use for an object you already have, that's "inside-the-box thinking." Another phrase that's inside the box: "Don't reinvent the wheel." Things that work well can be used as they are, but they can also be subtracted from, divided up, multiplied, unified, and dependent.

The *Wimpy Kid* books started with fewer words (subtraction), a series (multiplication), amusing kids while keeping them reading (task unification), and combined diary entries with pictures (attribute dependency). *Inside the Box* probably changed my life because it helped me see the kind of thinking that I was already engaged in as a designer at Poptropica, as an author, and now, as a bookstore owner.

Jeff Kinney is the author of Diary of a Wimpy Kid; *the creative and editorial director of Poptropica.com, which he founded; and the owner of An Unlikely Story Bookstore in Plainview, Massachusetts, where he lives with his wife and their sons.*

JULIE KLAM

on *Marjorie Morningstar*
by Herman Wouk

"Having a big fat book to read seemed so grown-up"

The title of my first book, a memoir, was *Please Excuse My Daughter*, because my mother and I loved to play hooky together and do things like shop and get our hair done. But the funny thing is, despite the way that might make her sound superficial, my mother is like the biggest reader of all time, and a very literary one. My mother always had her head in a book. Always. She would go to the library once a week and come home with like nine books. She's still like that. She comes here and takes all of my galleys and advance copies because she reads so much.

If you were trying to get my mother's attention about something, you used to have to smack her book closed! People think it's so terrible today with people's faces in their cell phones and tablets, but my mother was like that with a book! She read at a stoplight! But I admired that when I was young, and I loved reading something that my mother had read when she was young.

Much unlike the way my own daughter is today—ahem, Violet.

But the first book that really spoke to me and showed me that I could find my own way as a reader was *Marjorie Morningstar* by Herman Wouk. It was in that crinkly library plastic, the cover a skyline of New York City, and since it was an old copy from our town library, every page stayed open, that kind of thing.

I started reading and it was like . . . It was the moment I became a reader. I took the whole summer to read it, a long time, but that's because I wasn't just sitting and reading; I had to go to camp and whatever the hell else. But that book! When I see it, I still have this feeling of the memory of seeing the book waiting for me on my night table and being like "Ah!" . . . you know, that sort of joy of "I get to read this book."

I found out much later that the book was really special to my mother, too. She was dating my father when the movie came out, and the theme song, "A Very Precious Love," was "their song." Because my father had the band play it on every date they went on until they got married; they thought it was hilarious, because everybody thinks their love is special. For me, the book was a connection to her upbringing, too, because the Venn diagrams of our childhoods didn't overlap. I was raised in Katonah, New York. There were no Jewish kids around. No Jewish families or neighborhoods. This book had all of that community that my mother had known growing up, and we bonded over it and talked about it a lot.

Plus having a big fat book to read seemed so grown-up. (Are you listening to this, Violet?) I needed to feel somehow older and more sophisticated, because I wasn't Natalie Wood in a little dress, the way you should have been in Westchester at the time. Not that I even knew about Natalie Wood!

My mother was so smart. There's not a lot of sex or smut in

Marjorie Morningstar. It was romantic but not threatening, at a time when a lot of books that my friends were handing around were full of people giving blow jobs or whatever. This was not like that.

In this novel, the heroine gets picked up at her apartment by a man wearing a dinner jacket. Maybe that old-fashioned stuff was what helped me get truly taken away by the story. You're reading kids' books and you're entertained, but you're not lost. And then, all of a sudden, you're reading this book and you have no idea that any time has passed. It rarely happens to me now, because I think I have become the most distracted person in the world, but if I had read that book on the subway, I would have passed my stop. Many times.

I had always hated reading in school, because I like to read at my own pace. Summer reading is such a magical thing. I mean when you're a kid; when you're a grown-up, you still have your job to go to in the summertime. I get weepy when Violet gets her summer reading list—the titles just take me back. She has to read ten books this summer, although I think she plans to throw in a few comic books.

Julie Klam wrote the memoir Please Excuse My Daughter, *the essay collections* You Had Me at Woof *and* Love at First Bark, *and* Friendkeeping. *She is a columnist at* DAME *magazine.*

NICHOLAS KRISTOF

on *Four Essays on Liberty*
by Isaiah Berlin

"There is a pluralism of values"

I think the books that really awoke my love for reading were the Freddy the Pig books by Walter Brooks, about a pig who was also a detective. They really were pretty magical and made me an ardent reader. I scoured all the public libraries for some of the more obscure ones and I must have read some of them twenty times over.

But the book that awoke the idea that has most shaped my adult life was *Four Essays on Liberty* by Sir Isaiah Berlin. I was really very powerfully influenced by his idea that there's a very deep human yearning for one answer, for a single yardstick. The fact is, there is no such yardstick. There is a pluralism of values, and the challenge for us humans is to choose among competing values that we respect and admire, rather than to find an answer that works for everyone at once.

That insight has worked very well for me in becoming a newspaper columnist, but there is more to it than that. One thing I've discovered in my focus on the marginalized in general and on women and women's rights in particular is that my accidental, direct encounters with individuals affect me much more powerfully than anything I read. I read a great deal about social injustice, but it's actually those interactions that change me. If that's so for me, then I have to think about my readers, too. Maybe my toolbox of skills as a journalist is not enough to galvanize others. That's led me to broaden my toolbox as much as I can, to use photos and social media and even videos along with text. It isn't easy to build bridges of compassion, and whatever we can do to make those bridges easier to build is worthwhile.

It's so easy for us to assume that the thinkers that matter are from this tiny sliver of elite, educated men; it was Virginia Woolf's idea, in *A Room of One's Own:* What if Shakespeare had had a sister who was just as talented? That really moved me. Woolf, of course, is absolutely right, and it's true not only of Shakespeare but of people living all over the world today. You might find an Einstein in a village in Somalia—but that Einstein won't have the chance to meet his or her potential, and the world won't benefit from his or her talent, if that Einstein doesn't live past childhood or receive the education needed to harness skills.

There's a great change in the modern world. About 90 percent of adults worldwide are now literate. That is such a difference, and while things are obviously still grossly inadequate, there is more of a chance than ever before in history for an incredibly talented girl somewhere in the world to go to school, get an education, and perhaps bloom in ways that will allow her ideas and insights to benefit all of us.

Nicholas Kristof, a New York Times *op-ed columnist, writes about human rights, women's rights, health, and global affairs. He is the author, with his wife, Sheryl WuDunn, of* Half the Sky *and* A Path Appears.

LISA LAMPANELLI

on *Eat, Pray, Love*
by Elizabeth Gilbert

"I had to think about how I wanted my life to be"

Reading is essential to me. Books provide the kind of peace and stillness I can't get anywhere else in my life, from anything else in this world. I read every day, and I always have a book at hand on my tablet or in my tote bag.

I don't keep a reading diary or any kind of list, but I have noticed that books seem to find me just when I need them to, and I'm not just speaking about getting a particular message, I mean getting that message just when I'm in a life stage where I can use it.

My first example for you is Jen Lancaster's *Bitter Is the New Black*. Listen, I love Jen's books, all of them, so much—in fact, she and I are now close friends and we spend vacation time together every summer. But when I read *Bitter*, her first collection of essays, I was in a really go-go time of my career, making tons of money as a comedian and businesswoman, spending everything I wanted and most of what I had. When I read what could happen to a young woman who hadn't planned and saved and lost it all? It really hit me. Then I kept reading, and I started laughing. This woman was as funny as any of my stand-up colleagues, and she helped me wake up and understand that I had to think about how I wanted my life to be in its worst-case scenario. Of course, if I have any luck at all, in my life's worst case, I'll have Jen close by to get me laughing again.

The next book came to me after a couple of big relationships ended for me. *Eat, Pray, Love* by Elizabeth Gilbert, well, I could have written it and called it *Eat, Drink, Cry*. Aren't you glad I didn't? The point is, I did not know how to negotiate my way through endings, through loss. I may not have a few months to spend in Italy, an ashram reservation, or a hot lover in Bali—but I can learn how to relish a good meal, I can spend a week at Kripalu on a retreat, and I can appreciate a handsome man. Most of all, I can find a way to move on and move forward, which is what I've done. I'm healthier and happier and more grounded than I've ever been, even after going through a divorce in 2014.

So what I'm reading now is perfect: *Solemate: Master the Art of Aloneness and Transform Your Life* by Lauren Mackler. Yes, right now I'm single. That doesn't mean I will always be. Mackler's book isn't about learning how to be all by yourself until the end of time. It's about how to be all right by yourself whenever and wherever you are, and that's something I had not learned before, how to be completely fine by myself and with myself. No one ever taught me that you could do that, especially as a woman, and it is a joy to figure out that even if you wind up in a great relationship, you can maintain your individual identity and not simply wind up nurturing someone else's.

I'm not sure which book will come along next at just the

right time for me, but I do know that I learn these life lessons through books in a way that doesn't happen with anything else. Again, I think it's because reading forces you to slow down and focus. Come to think of it, that is a pretty good life lesson. And you read it right here.

Lisa Lampanelli is an American comedian and stand-up comic. She was on The Celebrity Apprentice *in 2012 and her memoir* Chocolate, Please: My Adventures in Food, Fat, and Freaks *was published in 2009.*

FRAN LEBOWITZ

on How Reading Is Her Life

"When it comes to books, I'm a gazillionaire"

Listen, if you wanted to find out which book changed my life, you should have asked me when I was six. I'm too old now to have anything change me.

I read all the time. All the time. That's what I do. It started when I was young and it has just never stopped. It drove my parents crazy. What I would do was, I would get a book and put it, open, in the top drawer of my desk. I would have my homework out on top, and since my mother was constantly shouting, "Are you doing your homework?" when she started coming down the hall I could just nudge the drawer shut with my belly and all she would see was my homework.

I was born in 1950. It was a different time. An earlier time. A simpler time, so simple that when I wanted to read my book in bed beneath the sheet with a flashlight, I had to borrow my father's flashlight, because children didn't have money then! Children weren't allowed to walk around with money. Also, children weren't allowed to do things that were too solitary or individual.

My parents urged me to go outside, play with others, and just come to the living room and watch TV with the family. The 1950s were all about community. If you liked being alone too much, there was something wrong with you.

Which may be why I also buy so many books. I never had money to buy them when I was younger. At some point in my twenties, when I was trying to make sure I had money for things like rent and food, I said, "When it comes to books, I'm a gazillionaire." I decided that I would always buy any books that I wanted, no matter what the price. It's not like I'm buying rare first editions, although at this point I do have a few of those. I buy books to read, and I read every day. All day.

This causes problems in Manhattan, real-estate problems. I have ten thousand books. I know this, because I just moved. Of course my new apartment has many bookshelves, and let me tell you, my books are kept in beautiful shelves, glass-fronted cabinets, the first editions right there along with the crumbly yellowing paperbacks. I do work with a private librarian, and we have all kinds of categories for my books, although he rightly insists that there shouldn't be a biography section because a person's biography should be shelved right along with her other books.

Much of my time used to be spent shopping for books. I remember when Fourth Street was just one secondhand bookstore after another, each filled to the ceiling with unreachable selections and each staffed by a grumpy Jewish man who usually sat out on the sidewalk and seemed reluctant to part with whichever book or books you actually wanted to buy. It was like an argument just to give him your money and go home with your treasures.

Sadly, there aren't very many bookstores anymore. These days I make most of my purchases at the Strand and the Argosy. If you ask me, the women who own the Argosy should be granted

Congressional Medals of Honor. They could sell for, and have been offered, many, many millions of dollars, but they refuse.

Listen, the Strand was great in the old days, but I am happy about their renovation because they put in air-conditioning. However, I'm not as interested in all of their sidelines. Tote bags are one thing, but chocolate bars at the cash register? I said to Fred, the owner then, "Why are there chocolate bars here? People can buy them at any corner bodega! I know people love chocolate, but I am here for the books!"

Frances Ann "Fran" Lebowitz is an American author and public speaker. Lebowitz is known for her sardonic social commentary on American life as filtered through her New York City sensibilities.

Yiyun Li

on *Dream Tales and Prose Poems*
by Ivan Turgenev

"You recognize yourself"

I grew up in a place where the library was not open to the public. So I'd never been in a library until I was twelve, when I was in middle school and allowed in as the library assistant. Since it was a school library, and a middle-school library at that, there were not that many good books.

But they had a copy of Turgenev's *Dream Tales and Prose Poems* in translation, and that's one of the most important books for me. It changed my whole everything. It changed my whole view of human nature, reading that book.

At twelve, you are at that age where you are really transitioning from being a child—and a young child; at least I was—and the nature of Turgenev's work is really gloomy, I would say. He was pessimistic about life. I did not, as a child, really understand him, but I absorbed that sense. Nobody in my life, in my immediate circle, would ever speak the truth about the way life was. No one would ever look at life and tell the truth about the way people treat each other and betray each other. History is so harsh, yet I wasn't hearing that acknowledged.

But Turgenev did. I read this title so many times that I about memorized it. At the time, I could recite many passages from the book. On thinking about this, I believe I read that book a little too early in life, because I was so young to become so gloomy. On the other hand, I'm grateful that I did read it then, because when you're young you absorb ideas so much more fully. It really established something for me.

We don't always choose when and how a book is going to change us. My rereadings of Turgenev? I know that I am going to a really deep place. I'm prepared for it, to some extent. But that first encounter was not by design.

Did Turgenev change my nature? Or did my nature, fully formed, respond to his work? For me, growing up, there was this imperative, an expectation that you must be positive. You must be happy. That's all I ever heard. And here's Turgenev, so gloomy, pessimistic, full of doom. That felt much closer to the real me than all the requirements in my culture to be happy.

Reading a book, the right book—you recognize yourself. It's not always cultivating a part of yourself, but rather paying attention to the self that is there. It has a right to exist. You have the right to feel gloomy or to look at things from a different angle. You know, even before I became a writer, I think that's what was most important for me as a human.

It's not that I'm so gloomy if you meet me. I don't want to sound like happiness is not important and laughter is not important. They are! But I'm drawn to this other side of things; I like to think about them. There was one Turgenev piece about a group of people talking, when a bug comes in and stings a young man, who then dies. I had heard about people dying, about executions, but no one explained them to me, and certainly they didn't explain them in this existential way Turgenev does.

Prose Poems has a lot of material about animals and the power of the natural world. There's one essay about two ancient mountains talking to each other, having a conversation about what they have seen. It sent me a strong moral message, not because Turgenev is a moralist—the poems contain a lot of ambivalence—but the message I got was that there is more to pay attention to than human happiness and positivity. There is another side of life. Maybe many sides. That was the mountain I wanted to try climbing in my own life, and eventually, in my own writing.

Yiyun Li grew up in Beijing and came to the United States in 1996. Her debut collection, A Thousand Years of Good Prayers, *won many awards, as did her novel* The Vagrants *and her second collection,* Gold Boy, Emerald Girl. Kinder Than Solitude, *her latest novel, was published to critical acclaim.*

LAURA LIPPMAN

on *Lolita*
by Vladimir Nabokov

"Nothing is out of reach"

I came to *Lolita* indirectly, through my sister, who read a lot of interesting humor writing when we were kids. When she was around fourteen and I was eleven or so, she was reading *Cold Comfort Farm* and *Please Don't Eat the Daisies.* One of Jean Kerr's pieces in *The Snake Has All the Lines* imagines a magazine feature called "Can This Marriage Be Saved?" if the couple were Humbert Humbert and Lolita.

I'm eleven and living in Baltimore, which means much of my life involves working backward without context. I don't know who Lolita is. I don't know what this is or why a column would be called "Can This Marriage Be Saved?" There were so many pop culture references that I didn't get. I lived in an old-fashioned world. I was laughing the other day because I still use the term "Fibber McGee's closet." No one says that anymore!

I connected the dots as I found them. I read this piece in my sister's book and I didn't get it, but what I did infer from it is that *Lolita* is a terrifically dirty book. I loved dirt. I still do. I loved dirty books when I was a kid and I was constantly on the lookout for the dirtiest books I could find. We kind of blame my mom, because she would read, say, *Valley of the Dolls* and hide it in the linen closet. Of course my sister found it, and she would go into this old-fashioned walk-in closet and stand there and read.

We were both avid for information from the adult world, and we thought we were getting it from books like *Valley of the Dolls* and *Peyton Place*. As we got older, in the 1970s, there were just so many terrifically nasty, dirty, smutty books. When I finally got my hands on *Lolita*, I was so disappointed at the lack of dirty parts.

However, the book stayed with me, and it's one I've gone back to again and again. It's a novel that forces you to ask yourself if certain subjects are taboo. Many smart, even scholarly people have said the book now makes them uncomfortable, because they don't believe that Nabokov could have known what he did about pedophilia if he did not have experience with it, or at the very least, suppressed desires.

That bothers me. I write about pretty horrific stuff. I wouldn't want people to draw the conclusion that because I imagine that stuff, I have experience with it, or suppressed desires to maim and kill and so on.

Also, I have reread *Lolita* fairly recently, and one of the things I think it's important to recognize is that this is a work written by one of the masters of the novel, someone who used language superbly. It's hard to believe there's a single unconsidered word or device in it, and so when I come to the moment where Nabokov breaks the "fourth wall" and lets Humbert slip that Lolita cries in the night, every night—that shows me that the author is letting you in on the fact that he understands the horror of what is happening, that Lolita, for all the sophistication Humbert believes he sees, is a little girl who cries in the bathroom every night.

That lets me know that as readers we were never supposed to lose sight of what was being done, that this is a child being violated. Humbert Humbert is wrong. Everything he offers up about himself and in his defense is erroneous.

So I think it's a book that can still be read. If a novelist thinks very hard about something and invests her full imagination into it, nothing is out of reach. It's interesting how little people talk about and value their imaginations. Whenever I meet someone who says, "I have no imagination," I ask, "What would do you if you won the lottery?" Everyone has an imagination, and although it may become a bit more reality bound as we grow older, peering inside someone else's imagination is always possible. Who could I have less in common with than Humbert Humbert? Yet through Nabokov's imaginative powers I am drawn into his story. His story—not Lolita's. I hope someday someone writes that one.

Laura Lippman is an award-winning, bestselling novelist whose works, including the Tess Monaghan detective series, often center around her home city of Baltimore, where she lives with her husband and daughter.

SARAH MACLEAN

on *The Great Gatsby*
by F. Scott Fitzgerald

"The person that I knew I wanted to be"

In a world that needs more decent men, Nick Carraway gives hope to me. I met him when I was about fifteen, in my AP literature class, and we'd just finished *The Scarlet Letter*, a book that I loathed. It captivated me from the very first, from the first page.

You're sort of thrown into this world, and at its core, it's a great story. On top of all its drama and intrigue, the language is simply beautiful. This novel is the reason I love New York City so much, but it's also the reason I think so much about relationships, both in my life and in my work, writing romance novels.

But if you set aside all the poetry and mythology and meaning, you have an unrequited love story that is just a layer on top of an examination of the ways in which we put our hopes and dreams on each other. We've all had our Daisy. We've all been Nick. Nick knows, from the start, that Gatsby can't win. Jay Gatsby is separate from everyone else, from the very beginning.

Imagine, too, being F. Scott Fitzgerald and writing *The Great Gatsby*—and never writing another book that comes close to its excellence. Artists often have to live with their best work being behind them. I mean, if you write *Gatsby*, you have to know you've written something that can't be surpassed. If you can't surpass yourself, you have to turn around and write something else.

But the book matters to me, terribly, because when I was a bit younger, at eleven, I was a real misfit and I fell in with a very bad crowd, because I wanted to feel like part of a group. We did some bad things, and I got in a lot of trouble, and I probably got in so much trouble that if my parents hadn't intervened, I would have gotten expelled and perhaps derailed from moving on with my life.

After that, I didn't make many friends at all. I really doubted the nature of friendship, because the people I'd thought were friends had steered me in the wrong direction. I withdrew, and I became a very quiet person who wasn't sure if she would ever have friends again. When I read *Gatsby*, Nick became my friend. I'm not exaggerating. He became my touchstone, the person that I knew I wanted to be, the person I might grow up to be, now that I was pointed in the direction that was right for me.

If I could just walk in Nick's shoes, things would happen, and life might be hard, but I would be honest, and true, and maybe I would find my way. Sometimes you need something to look up to, and for me, it wasn't going to be Daisy, who says that if she has a daughter, she wants her to be "a beautiful little fool."

Nick is an honorable man. I wanted to be an honorable person. Fitzgerald wrote a hero in Nick, and whenever I sit down and write one of my books, my heroes always wind up being Nick Carraway.

Before you wonder what a book might look like if one of the

heroines were Nick Carraway—well, I've written that book, or really, books. It's a four-book series called *The Rules of Scoundrels*, and I don't want to completely spoil it, but the final novel is titled *Never Judge a Lady by Her Cover*. Heroines are good people, too. Most of the heroines in romance novels, to tell you the truth, are also Nick Carraway.

Sarah MacLean is the New York Times, Washington Post, *and* USA Today *bestselling author of historical romance novels that have been translated into more than twenty languages. She is also the winner of back-to-back RITA Awards for best historical romance from the Romance Writers of America.*

GREGORY MAGUIRE

on *The Once and Future King*
by T. H. White

"Audacity is the great propellant"

At around fifteen or sixteen I was beginning to be interested in musical theater, and I loved *Camelot*. As a gay teenager, musical comedies and their cast recordings meant a huge amount to me. (I've never entirely understood why.) I also admired the Disney film *The Sword in the Stone*, and when I realized the two creations had been inspired by the same story, I thought, "I can't just let this sit. I have to find it."

So, instead of finding Chrétien de Troyes, I sought out T. H. White's novel *The Sword in the Stone*. It was a mass-market paperback that cost ninety-five cents, and I read and reread it so often that I still remember one of the cover blurbs: "Read it and laugh. Read it and learn. Read it and be glad you are human."

The novel was funny but also true, profound, sad, sympathetic. So of course my waggish high school friend and I used that quote over and over to describe everything from my sister's third-grade book report to a comic strip in the Sunday newspaper. We thought we were so superior. I did not see until later that some contemporary readers might even apply such a blurb to *Wicked*. My subconscious must have gotten out its stenographer's pad when I was reading White!

The point is this: I really was reading to learn, and what I learned is that audacity is the great propellant. By writing his books about the Arthurian legend, T. H. White basically said, "I don't give a flying fig about de Troyes or Mallory or anybody else's version. I'm going to write about what the story means to me. And I'm going to do it as it's never been done before."

I'd published a lot of children's books before I wrote *Wicked*. When the idea for the novel came to me, I knew I wanted to tell the story of *The Wizard of Oz* as if no one had ever heard of it before. And I knew it would have to be a book I wrote with audacity—because it was to be about evil, and the last place you'd expect to find a serious exploration of evil is in a children's book. For children, evil and good are black and white. It's only once we're adults that we get to play with the idea that things might not be so crisply delineated. We owe it to our fellow human beings to slow down a little bit before we start slinging around insults. Delimiting someone by a single word, like "wicked" or "beautiful," isn't accurate or just. If you're going to be just, you have to be cautious.

I have a doctorate in literature, and my dissertation was about how the first golden age of fantasy for children, from 1865 or so, when Lewis Carroll wrote *Alice's Adventures in Wonderland*, was shattered by the horrors of World War I. That was the end of childhood as a time of unalterable innocence.

But good came out of this: in the late 1930s, as Europeans shuddered at the darkness of Nazism in Germany and Stalinism in the Soviet Union, two books were released. One was Tolkien's *The Hobbit*, and the other was White's *The Sword in the Stone*. These books, written with such close attention to their contemporary events, kind of broke the mold and made fantasy an adult genre, too. It conferred dignity to the expansive possibilies inherent in fantasy, as a literary genre—evoking the seriousness even, I'd suggest, of someone like Dante, who used a huge metaphor and fantastic ideas to make serious points about our lives and our struggles and the world.

White wrote four other books about Arthur that were collected and released as *The Once and Future King*. By the time he finished, World War II was raging. As I recall, the last lines of *The Book of Merlyn*, which was published after he died, were: "Here your humble servant Terence Hanbury White lays down his pen and picks up his sword to go fight for his country."

What is *The Once and Future King* about if not the misuse of power and might? And if there's a misuse, then there must also be a correct use. The long biography of Arthur starts with the child Wart being turned into a fish by Merlin the Magician, and it ends with one of the most important ideas about being human. How do we use the strength we have, and how do we deal with people who are not as strong as we are? From fish to feeling. That's magical.

Gregory Maguire's books include Wicked, Confessions of an Ugly Stepsister, *and, most recently,* After Alice. *He lives with his husband and their three children in Massachusetts.*

JUDITH MARTIN

on *The Image*
by Daniel Boorstin

"His ideas just electrified me"

When I heard this question, I knew immediately which book I would choose. It's *The Image* by Daniel Boorstin. Boorstin is one of our most original American thinkers, and he's not read as widely as he should be today, so it may not be easy to explain what an impact *The Image* had on our culture when it was published in 1962.

I began my career at the *Washington Post*, and I spent twenty-five years there as a journalist covering what was too long known as "the women's beat." I was a reporter, feature writer, and critic for the sections that eventually became known as Style and Weekend. I knew, and so did many of my colleagues, that reporting was changing. But it took Boorstin, with that wonderful subtitle *A Guide to Pseudo-Events in America*, to pinpoint the change.

Boorstin understood that we had started to mistake the illusion for reality, meaning that the more contrived and staged something was, the more we believed in it. I know a lot about theater, both as a drama critic and as someone who writes about costume and stage sets, and his ideas just electrified me. He said that pseudo-events were leading to pseudo-people—also known as "celebrities." This was back in the early 1960s! He predicted the advent of people like the Kardashian family, who are famous simply for being famous.

While Daniel Boorstin was worried about high culture being ruined by the masses, we journalists were worried about facts being obscured by puppetry, and we were right to be worried. Look what happened just a decade later—Watergate. He worried about American ideals, and so did we, in the media, but we weren't as concerned with things like lofty intellect. We were more concerned with the truth.

The amazing thing is that you can arrive at a truth many ways. Boorstin wrote about the Kennedy-Nixon debate and warned about the dangers of a candidate being packaged so perfectly that you don't actually listen to his message—or listen to his opponent's message, either. That's more of a danger now than it was in 1962.

Artifice has its place, which Boorstin either didn't understand or was terrified of as an idea. Miss Manners, for example, is a persona, not a person. But Miss Manners would never try to run a country, or even your life. That would be rude. But sometimes people want an imitation or a heightened experience. The thing that Boorstin and I would agree on is that it should be presented as such. No one should believe the hype, even if it's beautiful and pleasant to experience. An excellent production can add to our appreciation of Shakespeare, but a production that looks and sounds and feels Shakespearean built around a commercial jingle isn't the same thing at all.

Boorstin recognized that the rise in pseudo-events could only lead to the rise of pseudo-manners, a way of fawning over characters with empty heads and emptier souls. Watergate happened, yes. But what also happened? Katharine Graham, Ben Bradlee, Carl Bernstein, and Bob Woodward banded together and made sure that Watergate was exposed and its like could not happen again.

Judith Martin, whose professional moniker is Miss Manners, has written numerous books on manners and etiquette. She began her career at the Washington Post, *where she spent over two decades refining that publication's Style and Weekend sections.*

ALEXANDER MCCALL SMITH

on *Collected Shorter Poems*
by W. H. Auden

"A completely satisfying philosophy of life"

I first came across the English poet W. H. Auden when I was living in Belfast. I had my first job, which was at Queen's University there, and I had found this book in the university library. I borrowed it, read it, and discovered all this poetry that I had never encountered prior to that.

But it was *Collected Shorter Poems*, which is a really marvelous introduction to his work, that changed my life. Those poems made me think about different aspects of life than I'd been accustomed to considering and introduced me to a wonderful, humane voice in the dormant world—or at least a world that felt dormant to me at the time.

I think possibly the poem that really impressed me in that initial reading was "In Memory of Sigmund Freud"; it moved me greatly. The lines about being enthusiastic over the night "because it needs our love" still affect me, and so do the lines of another poem, "In Praise of Limestone," where Auden holds something up for its evanescence. Those two really stood out the first time I read his work.

"In Praise of Limestone" is such a surprising poem. It's about a rock, which is not an obviously normal topic. And that's one of Auden's great talents. He could write about things like old machinery, or geology, or an academic subject, or even war, and make it poetic, find the humanity in it. But I think that what really touches me about that poem is where he talks about how changeable desire is: "when I try to imagine a faultless love / Or the life to come, what I hear is the murmur / Of underground streams, what I see is a limestone landscape."

With Auden's poems, I think it's often the case that there is a very, very small number of words or a single line that says so much. "Lay your sleeping head, my love / Human on my faithless arm." And, of course, "If equal affection cannot be / Let the more loving one be me." There's an entire philosophy, a completely satisfying philosophy of life, right there. Auden was a devout Anglican, but I think his personal creed is one of protectiveness and appreciation of the other that transcends cultures and religious boundaries.

Over the years I've given that a great deal of thought, because I do read Auden frequently. Not every day, but every couple of weeks. I take out my copy, which is still the one from my Belfast days, although I now have a quite lovely one somebody thought to give me on the shelf, too. I also do recommend *Collected Shorter Poems* to others, not simply for their education, but because these poems are important to who I am.

I'll read a poem or three until I feel a sense of quiet, or begin to ponder something from his words in my own way. One way to explain why this is important to me is to share another book central to my life, *The Odes of Horace*. I never tire of them, and I find so much wisdom and power in them—but they do not bring me a sense of peace the way Auden does.

Perhaps there was something about the period in which he lived, seeing as a boy the last rays of England's "golden afternoon," then watching men return from the First World War in physical and psychological tatters, living through the decades in which Europe marched toward another and even more terrible war. Perhaps it has to do with the intersection of his sexual orientation and his religious faith. Perhaps it is his intellect and curiosity in the face of those things and more; he was a complicated man who did not have an easy or simple life. But Auden, again and again, never as a bore, reminds us that life ends, life goes on, life decays, love endures. In "September 1, 1939": "We must love one another or die."

Alexander McCall Smith, author of The No. 1 Ladies' Detective Agency *series, the Isabel Dalhousie mysteries, and the* 44 Scotland Street *serial, published* Emma, *in 2014, a reimagining of the Jane Austen classic. His latest release is* The Novel Habits of Happiness, *an Isabel Dalhousie book.*

ELIZABETH
MCCRACKEN

on *Borrowed Time*
by Paul Monette

"It shattered me, that book"

I thought a lot about this question. It's such a good one. There have been so many books that changed my life in small and large ways—for a while I was toying with saying Clement Wood's *Rhyming Dictionary*, because it's one of the first reference books I remember reading for pleasure, and going through it is the first time I really remember being thunked over the head by the joy of language.

But in the end I think the answer is Paul Monette's *Borrowed Time*. I took it out from the Iowa City Public Library's new-book shelf early in my first year in graduate school, in 1988, the year it was published. I still remember sitting in my ugly orange armchair, reading it. I'd never sobbed at a book before and I've never sobbed since.

I certainly understood how important it was as I read it. Really, it taught me about romantic love in a way, as well as about loss—it's about Monette's partner's illness with and death from AIDS, and I think I'd never read anything that seemed so full of love in a way I understood was realistic, actual, unflinching, beautiful, upsetting: what you suffered through when somebody you loved was both suffering and going away from you. It shattered me, that book. I'm not sure I really knew a book could do that.

I also didn't know anything about AIDS until then, apart from on the newspaper-reading, abstract level.

I have never reread it. I've thought about rereading. I even toyed with teaching it last year in my memoir class, but then I realized that if even one of my students didn't like *Borrowed Time*, it was over between me and that student. It's really important to me that students can feel whatever they like about a book I teach, and there are plenty of books I adore that can withstand the scorn of students. But not loving that book—I couldn't stand it.

Until you asked, I would have said that the book didn't really get into my writerly brain, it so shook me on the spiritual level. But it was probably right about then that I really began to write about loss in my fiction, long before I ever had any firsthand experience of it. I suppose reading *Borrowed Time* made me think nothing else could ever be so meaningful. Eventually, alas, my life caught up with my interest.

Weirdly, I've never owned a copy of *Borrowed Time*. I should probably fix that. It was a time when I was reading all the time, lots of books that were important to me (I read *The Heart Is a Lonely Hunter* in that same chair, that same year); I didn't own any of them. I grew up in a public library. Only when I grew old and greedy did I really care about owning books I read.

I don't know if people still read it. Yes, I think they should, but on the other hand I need to read it again, too.

Elizabeth McCracken is the author of five books: the story collection Here's Your Hat What's Your Hurry, *the novels* The Giant's House *and* Niagara Falls All Over Again, *the memoir* An Exact Replica of a Figment of My Imagination, *and* Thunderstruck & Other Stories.

GAIL MCGOVERN

on *Green Eggs and Ham*
by Dr. Seuss

"Try the change"

My role model is Clara Barton herself. She has a quote that I have hanging behind my desk: "I have almost complete disregard for precedent . . . I go for anything new that might improve the past."

With that as background, the most important book to me is *Green Eggs and Ham* by Dr. Seuss. My parents first read it to me when I was a child, and I remember my mother actually scrambled eggs with blue food coloring to turn them green; I don't think she managed to tint the ham, but my memory may be faulty. In any case, she says I then told her, "I *do* like green eggs and ham!"

It's sort of become this mantra for me. You can try new things as a leader. You have to embrace change and you also have to course-correct when a change you've implemented doesn't work. The American Red Cross is a 134-year-old institution. When I got here, we were kind of a twentieth-century delivery vehicle. Now we have well over two million Twitter followers. We use social media tracking to find out where help is needed; we even have kids in their jammies using GPS to guide us to crisis points. There is a culture here that has learned how to change, but more important, when people try something and it's a bust, they'll try something else.

A great example of that was during Hurricane Sandy. The disaster was so enormous; it impacted fourteen different states, and we needed lots of volunteers. We had tapped into our partners and our own reserves and we weren't sure where to turn. But when the storm cleared, we received a huge and spontaneous outpouring of requests to volunteer from people who were local to affected areas.

Normally it's a long process to become a Red Cross volunteer, but this was a once-in-a-lifetime opportunity. We said, let's process people really quickly. We set up a tablet-based intake process where background and training took just twenty minutes total. We would put these volunteers, say, on an assembly line to give out water—we weren't putting people into situations where they didn't have proper skills. But we found it made a real difference in communities. Places heal faster when community members participate in recovery.

The thing is, we couldn't have done that before. Sandy was a kind of defining moment for our organization because social media was lighting everything up, and we learned from the process. We've now got apps under development so we can send out emergency tips; we've had 7.9 million downloads. If an organization naturally welcomes change and people aren't wedded to just one way of doing things, then we can take these new tools and use them to make things better for millions of people.

When my mother read *Green Eggs and Ham* to me and I said, "I don't like green eggs and ham," she said, "Try it. Try the green eggs," and she made them for me and I discovered something.

Try the change. That's what I learned.

Gail McGovern is president and CEO of the American Red Cross. Recognized twice by Fortune *magazine as one of the top fifty most powerful women in corporate America, she also serves on numerous boards of directors, including the board of Johns Hopkins Medicine.*

DAVID MITCHELL

on *The Wind-up Bird Chronicle*

by Haruki Murakami

*"A master class in harnessing the spirit of
'anything could happen next'"*

I was living in Japan. I had gone from being in a private language
school with a sort of built-in social network to a big, elderly, drafty
university that employed exactly one foreigner—and that was
me. My conservative new employer had hired me as an attempt to
rebrand itself as a new international academy, and I was the "international" part. I was teaching just a few classes each week, but
as with many Japanese social contexts, the important thing was to
be seen to be there, even if you had no real work to do.

    This is really where I wrote my first two novels. I was also
somewhat lonely, as my girlfriend (and future Mrs. Mitchell) could
only meet up with me on weekends. My main form of weekday
entertainment, then, was reading. To be honest, it's the last period
in my life when I had enough reading time, and it was during this

time in my life that I discovered Murakami. My girlfriend was a great reader (she still is), and she got me reading him before he was famous outside of Japan. I'd finished *Ghostwritten* and was thinking about a second book. She told me how important he was in Japan, how he was read by occasional as well as regular readers, and how he had a fresh, immediate, unpretentious and fluid style of writing.

What struck me back then was how Murakami was both a self-effacing writer who had no interest in being lionized by the literary scene in Japan, and yet despite this (or because of it?) he had also been appointed as a sort of moral compass for Japan. A lesser example is his inclusion of the wartime Japanese client state in Manchukuo in *The Wind-Up Bird Chronicle* (a historical embarrassment rarely discussed even now), while a major example is Murakami's book *Underground*, a nonfiction collection of interviews with survivors of the Aum Shinrikyo sarin gas attack on the Tokyo metro in 1995. While pundits, politicos, and (stunningly) apologists for these murderous death-cult nut-jobs filled the media with opinions and counter-opinions, Murakami simply, calmly, and humanely went round from house to house and let people tell their story in their own words. What a dignified and useful thing for a writer to do in the face of a national atrocity.

Still, it is Murakami the Novelist rather than Murakami the Public Figure who influenced me most, back in the day, especially in terms of his attitude to literary risk. *The Wind-up Bird Chronicle* is a prodigiously risky book, which could easily be a total dog's dinner, but instead it's a strange and beautiful masterpiece unlike anything I'd ever read. It jumps about in time, it has sub-realities, it sends its protagonist down a dry well—I mean, what dead end is deader than the bottom of a dry well? And yet, the well turns out not to be a dead end at all—or dry. Murakami is an admirer of *Twin Peaks*, and he's sort of got that Lynchian spirit of anything can happen. In unskilled hands that spirit is a false friend who makes novels ill-disciplined and poorly focused, but *The Wind-Up Bird Chronicle* is a master class in harnessing the spirit of "anything could happen next" and putting it to spectacular use.

As the newest employee at my backwater university, I had the worst office with only half a window and one old sofa and not much else, but I had Haruki Murakami. During the long stretches of the day when I wasn't teaching, I'd lie on the sofa, utterly engrossed in Murakami's anonymous, magic-limned Japan. I thought, *God, I want to write like this.* My literary crush is evident in my second novel *number9dream*, set completely in Japan, with a long historical interlude, a strange multi-layered plot, a kind of hardboiled loneliness, and a collision between the realist world and a supernatural one—all Murakami's tropes. Did *The Wind-Up Bird Chronicle* change my life? No, but it did change my approach to writing by demonstrating what happens when a writer is unswervingly faithful to an eccentric vision. Don't worry about guessing or second-guessing what you are told the market wants, or what you fear reviewers might say, or what a writer at this stage of your career should be publishing. In art, if not in gunfights, it is better to aim at audacity and fail than aim at mediocrity and succeed. To your novel's finest self, be true.

David Mitchell is the award-winning and bestselling author of Slade House, The Bone Clocks, The Thousand Autumns of Jacob de Zoet, Black Swan Green, Cloud Atlas, number9dream, *and* Ghostwritten. *Twice shortlisted for the Man Booker Prize, Mitchell was named one of the 100 most influential people in the world by* Time *in 2007. With KA Yoshida, Mitchell translated from Japanese the internationally bestselling memoir* The Reason I Jump. *He lives in Ireland with his wife and two children.*

BRAD MELTZER

on *Justice League of America* #150

"The greatness that all of us can achieve"

The book that changed my life was *Justice League of America* #150, published in 1978. I think I was seven years old. And it wasn't the first comic book I ever got. But it was the first one I ever remember reading by myself, cover to cover.

I'm almost positive this copy was bought by my father, a major sports fan who would rather have bought a baseball—but he used to manage a greeting-card store in Penn Station, and on his way home, he always brought me a handful of comic books. Plus, it was the Justice League: Superman, Batman, Wonder Woman, Green Lantern…they were all there.

What I remember distinctly was one page where all of the heroes are trapped in prisons shaped like keyholes—because they were fighting a villain called The Key, naturally. At age seven that seemed absolutely logical to me. The prisons were stacked on top of one another, three or four rows wide, a giant bunch of heroes, and none of them could move. I don't even remember what the reason was that The Key had captured everyone.

"Oh God, what's going to happen to them?" I thought, at seven. I was terrified.

From there, two things happened that forever affected how I write. You can see what I learned in this comic book in just about every book I write today

Each hero can't escape from his (or her) prison because it's built to the specifications of their weakness. Kryptonite for Superman, a yellow glow for Green Lantern, you can imagine the rest. But The Flash realizes he can vibrate—and therefore move from his prison to the one next to him. A few vibrations later, he's in the same prison as the Elongated Man. Are you still with me? Have your eyes glazed over from a cloud of nerdiness? They shouldn't, because this was amazing!

So now, Elongated Man stretches his body into a treadmill. Get it? A treadmill. Something that Flash can run on. And from there, Flash runs so fast, it cracks open all the other prisons.

This is 1978, in full Silver Age of comics madness. However, there's one unmistakable message in this insanity, this beautiful insanity: The only way you get out of anything is by working together. That was catnip for me, the idea that Superman couldn't do it, Batman couldn't do it, The Flash couldn't do it, but if they worked *together*, they could do anything (including escape).

At seven, I had a fair amount of friends—but I didn't have the friends I really wanted, friends like me, who liked comics, who liked to read, who liked to figure out puzzles and mysteries and the like. When I read *Justice League* #150, I thought: "If I had the kinds of friends who were like me, we certainly could do anything together."

But the second lesson is just as important to me. The villain in the book turns out to be Snapper Carr (because he walked around snapping his fingers; again, the Silver Age of Comics, remember?). Snapper is sort of a Justice League mascot, a teenager who hangs out with them. When they discover he's betrayed them, that he's working against his own friends, well, that was just devastating.

Heroes, you see—they're exactly like us. History books tend to put people like Abraham Lincoln and Rosa Parks up on pedestals. They're treated as gods. But know this: No one is born a hero. We're all born the same way, and we have to achieve and work hard and struggle and fight. But if we teach our kids that the power of people like Lincoln and Parks is inside all of us, that each one of us has the potential to do something great, that could change the world. And it doesn't have to be about something history making. It could just be about helping one person, being kind to one person. That's the greatness that all of us can achieve.

Brad Meltzer is the author of The Inner Circle, The Book of Fate, *and seven other bestselling thrillers. His newest thriller is* The President's Shadow. *His newest children's book is* I Am Helen Keller. *Oh, and he also wrote a comic book:* Justice League of America.

KATE MULGREW

on *The Country Girls*
by Edna O'Brien

"I peeked through that wonderful curtain of a story"

All of us in my large Irish Catholic family were voracious readers. We'd go to the library every week and my mother had a big burlap bag and we'd fill it to the brim with our selections, including hers.

Every day from two o'clock to two forty-five p.m. was my mother's reading time, and it really was reading time, not an excuse for a nap. That stretch was sacrosanct for her. Not only did it teach me that reading was important and worth your time, I knew there was an active process going on in that room, a mysterious and exalting thing that uplifted and advanced her.

We didn't have a TV, so books were our entertainment. My mother would shepherd me through a certain author—for example, Willa Cather. She suggested I start with *My Ántonia*, and I remember it as the first time I peeked through that wonderful curtain of a story and couldn't tell where it left off and I began. I fell in love with Tony, that headstrong bold young girl, and the way she saw prairie life. I loved *War and Peace* for the scope and saga, and *Remembrance of Things Past* for its singular voice and style.

But of late I've been changed by Edna O'Brien, the doyenne of Irish literature and surely the most gifted woman now writing in English. Her trilogy *The Country Girls* has that quality her stories do, when she speaks to me with her magic and her darkness and her delicacy and her wit and her mist she rises out of. She does that exquisite thing I seem to respond to in writers, which is that she hides the diamond. You must find it yourself. She will not reveal anything in a blatant way. It's the most gorgeous, subtle, torturous thing. Her marriage was a disaster, but you will never see that revealed. She will dance around it, she will linger at the gate, she will let you see a bit of that tragic union beckoning distantly, but she will not spell it out for you.

I think I'm so entranced by O'Brien because her spirit is still deeply enmeshed, entrenched, embedded in the Irish way of life. It's in the depth of her relationship with her mother, in the unresolved harshness of daily life there, in the love of the land, the magic of the Irish people, and the fickleness of their religion, too.

Yet Ireland reviled her. She was roundly despised for committing adultery and leaving her marriage and she wound up living and writing in London. But she never lost her essential Irish nature, and she continued to write impeccably about the very thing that has divided Ireland for all time. It's hidden and strange and backward, especially in a people who may in some ways be the most advanced in the world spiritually, but the thing that divides Ireland is how women are viewed.

O'Brien shows in her novels and short stories and even in her recent memoir that women have been stifled and viewed as mediocre, sort of less than human, for so long in Ireland that for some generations the wound was gangrenous. Any time a woman took for herself—the best biscuit, a lover, a job—she was seen as monstrous, unnatural, indefensible. So my mother's afternoon time with her library books was truly an act of revolution for a new-world woman of Irish heritage. Give us this day our daily read, you know?

Kate Mulgrew is an actor best known for playing Captain Janeway on Star Trek: Voyager *and Galina "Red" Reznikov on* Orange Is the New Black. *Her memoir* Born with Teeth *was published in 2015.*

CELESTE NG

on *Harriet the Spy*
by Louise Fitzhugh

"So great on so many levels"

Oh, how I loved to read when I was a child. Is everyone saying this?

I read everything I could get my hands on, but the book that stands out for me is *Harriet the Spy* by Louise Fitzhugh, and I can't believe no one has picked this one already because it's so great on so many levels.

First, Harriet is basically a free-range child. Her parents don't worry much about her. She's eleven, she lives on the Upper East Side in Manhattan, and she has a nanny named Ole Golly who is in charge of her care and her psyche, as far as I could tell.

Second, Harriet knows tragedy and loss. The book's plot hinges on the fact that Ole Golly, maker of endless tomato sandwiches and layer cakes, has accepted the marriage proposal of one Mr. Waldenstein and is about to leave, telling Harriet and her parents that Harriet is old enough to take care of herself. Harriet isn't so sure, and when her beloved and secret notebook gets stolen from the school playground, things go from bad to worse.

Third—and this is most important to me—the book is called *Harriet the Spy*, and she is supposedly spying on all of these friends. But what Harriet is really doing as she scribbles in her notebook is learning how to become a writer. Everything in her notebook is completely honest—and sometimes that means it isn't very nice. She tells the truth as she sees it without thinking about other people's feelings.

That's what novelists do. That's what novelists have to do. If we fiction writers stopped to consider everyone's feelings, we'd never finish a sentence, let alone an entire manuscript, and we certainly wouldn't be able to see our words published. It's not that there aren't consequences—Harriet certainly learns that lesson—and each of us has to negotiate our own way of responding to those. Some people allow those close to them who are reflected in a book to read it, or read certain pages. Some people change names and identifying details. Some people just go for broke and don't worry about it.

The main thing Harriet M. Welsch taught me was that the art of observing must be undertaken alone. It's great to have friends, and I loved that Harriet and her friends were quirky, real-seeming kids, not fairy-tale versions of children, but even if you have friends, you are responsible for what you do, and your version of things isn't wrong just because it isn't nice and neat and tidy. So much of writing involves learning to see and listen and experience.

Remember the part of the book where Ole Golly tells Harriet she has to do two things and she doesn't like either one of them? Ole Golly says that if Harriet wants to make things right, she has to apologize—and she has to lie. "Otherwise, you are going to lose a friend." I think of that again and again as I write and revise and publish and read and write again. We have to decide which friends are worth these acts. But, but, but: thank goodness Harriet has already learned how to observe. I hate to think of what she might be like if she started out apologizing and lying. I'm glad she started out telling the truth.

Celeste Ng is the author of the novel Everything I Never Told You, *which was a* New York Times *bestseller, a* New York Times *Notable Book, and Amazon's number one Best Book of the Year 2014. A recipient of a Pushcart Prize, she lives in Cambridge, Massachusetts.*

SUSAN ORLEAN

on *The Sound and the Fury*
by William Faulkner

*"People care very much, really fervently,
about the books that matter to them"*

My family was on vacation in Jamaica, and somehow I'd brought a copy of *The Sound and the Fury* by William Faulkner. I was in the ninth grade, and I'd been an avid reader, but I'd never read a book like this. I was utterly absorbed and sucked into the world of Yoknapatawpha County, to the point that I couldn't leave the hotel room. My family kept saying, "Come out to the beach!" And I thought: "I can't. I have to stay in this book."

Of course, my parents were mad at me, but this novel consumed me so much that I began rereading it before I'd even finished my first read, so I was reading in two different places! This was the point where I started to read more the way I needed to, digging into literature in a different way. Feeling the transformational power of a book was world-changing for me.

The combination of the depth of emotion in the book and

the mastery of the writing floored me. There's no dovetail to my own life; I didn't come to it with any connections to or preexisting interest in the South. But it is the story of a family, the tides that find and sometimes strangle that family, and the presence of history in the life of a family.

So it changed my life, and my perspective, and, I hope, my own writing—at least a little. But years later, *The Sound and the Fury* wound up playing a different kind of life-changing role for me. I was living in Manhattan, and I had been fixed up on a blind date. I was very skeptical, because here I was, a writer and a reader, and at the time he was an investment banker. I thought, "Oh my God, we have nothing in common. He's a money guy. I'm a word person."

But I went. And in the middle of our dinner, I don't remember how it came up, but one of us mentioned *The Sound and the Fury* and we both lit up, both said this was the one book that meant the most to us. It turns out that my date, now my husband, was something of an independent Faulkner scholar. He had read all of his books, and planned to get a doctorate and write his dissertation on Faulkner before life led him elsewhere.

It was just so funny and unexpected. Are you kidding me? We wound up, obviously, on a second date, and many subsequent dates. We even went away on several weekends together where we each brought a copy of *The Sound and the Fury* and had our own kind of book club.

My first copy, a paperback, is lost to time, but I do still have a two-volume biography of Faulkner that is signed by Joseph Blotner, with whom I studied in college. I remember that Blotner worked on that book for at least twenty years, and a few years back, when I was reading another big fat biography by someone else, I thought about how the book that changed my life made me want to read Blotner's great work. So I casually tweeted something like "What were your world-changing books?"

What followed was national. It was an explosion, a classic case of something going viral. There were thousands of responses, and the thrill to me was realizing that books matter, both as people relate to them and as people share the effect they had. It was really very thrilling, I think, to those of us who have been in the world of publishing for the last twenty years. There's this deep sense of being sidelined anachronisms. Then you see that even though technology has changed the way books are created, delivered, and sold, people care very much, really fervently, about the books that matter to them.

Fervently. My husband and I just went to see a performance by an innovative theater company in New York City called the Elevator Repair Service. They put on a version of *The Sound and the Fury*. It continues to play a role in our lives.

Susan Orlean is an American journalist and author. Her books include The Orchid Thief, The Bullfighter Checks Her Makeup, *and* Rin Tin Tin. *She has been a staff writer for* The New Yorker *since 1992.*

RUTH OZEKI

on *The Pillow Book*
by Sei Shonagon

"The writer and the reader are in conversation"

When I first thought about this question, what came to mind were early childhood books like *Charlotte's Web* and *Harriet the Spy*, and later *Little Women* and *Jane Eyre*, the books that make little girls want to become writers. But then I remembered a book that both influenced me during a formative period of my life and then stayed with me, and one that I still revisit from time to time, like an old friend. So I'd have to say the book that changed my life would be *The Pillow Book* by Sei Shonagon.

Sei Shonagon was a gentlewoman who served the Empress Teishi in the Heian court of Japan, over a thousand years ago. I first read *The Pillow Book* in high school, in a Japanese history or culture class at Concord Academy. I must have been fifteen or sixteen, and I felt an immediate sense of connection, like Sei Shonagon and I had something in common. The idea of a teenage girl in the 1970s having something in common with a tenth-century Japanese courtier sounds crazy, but I really did feel like I knew her.

Of course there were plenty of arcane references to life in the Heian court that I didn't get at all, but what struck me about her writing, and what I responded to, was its intimacy. She writes in an informal, colloquial style to an audience she knew well, the people of the imperial court, and she simply assumes her readers will be familiar with the details of her world. This tone of hers, with its casual assumption of familiarity, is irresistible, and it sweeps you along, even if you're a teenager wearing love beads and shredded bell-bottoms.

Which brings me to something else I felt we had in common: Sei Shonagon was a contrarian, and as a teenager, so was I—or at least I was trying very hard to be. She was very aware that even though her readers knew and shared a world, they might not agree with her opinions and assessments of it; in fact, she assumed they wouldn't, and she didn't care. I loved this!

She had very strong opinions, and at that age, I thought it was important to have strong opinions, too. She was arrogant, prescriptive, and a bit of a showoff, but she was also very wry and funny. And she was an intellectual snob. She read and wrote men's literary Japanese, which showed a flaunting of conventional sex and gender roles that seemed thrillingly transgressive to me—not what you'd think of when you think of a Japanese court lady—and as a nascent feminist, I thought all of this was pretty cool. She had lots of lovers and could be quite critical of them, and I thought this was very funny. Of course, at that age I was very interested in the subject of lovers, too.

And then there was the poetry. People in the Heian court took their poetry very seriously, and Sei Shonagon's poetic awareness of beauty and transience, infused by Buddhist teachings of impermanence, spoke to me as an adolescent and continues to speak to me today.

On my website, I've got a sidebar next to my weblog that says, "If Sei Shonagon had had access to the Internet, she would've had a blog instead of a pillow book," and I think that's true. *The Pillow Book* is a kind of genre-bending miscellany, which feels very contemporary. It's like a diary or a journal. She writes in fragments and creates a kind of montage, moving back and forth between opinions, fact and fiction, little stories, and of course her famous lists: Rare Things; Squalid Things; Things That Make the Heart Beat Faster. How can you not love that? Our lists, our taxonomies, shape the way we experience the world.

This approach to writing intrigued me, and I realize now that I adopted these kinds of techniques, writing in fragments and keeping the fragments suspended until they resolve, starting way back with my early film work. And I certainly used them in *My Year of Meats* and *A Tale for the Time Being*. In fact, Sei Shonagon is almost a character in *My Year of Meats*, a ghostly figure who haunts the periphery of the novel and occasionally intrudes into the consciousness of the two protagonists, Jane Takagi-Little and Akiko Ueno.

And I just realized something else, too. I said earlier that Sei Shonagon's *Pillow Book* is like a journal, but *unlike* a journal or diary, it seems to assume a reader, an unspecified "you" with whom the writer is in conversation. This assumption of a "you" is what creates the intimate tone, the sense of connection between writer and reader, and this is exactly what's happening with Nao's diary in *A Tale for the Time Being*. Nao is writing in her diary with the expectation that someone will find it and read it. The work is transitive by nature; the writer and the reader are in conversation and inextricably interconnected. This interconnectedness is another

Buddhist philosophical teaching at the heart of *A Tale for the Time Being*, so maybe you could even say that Sei Shonagon was my first Buddhist teacher!

But putting all this literary and philosophical stuff aside, what I love most about *The Pillow Book* is the way it reveals Sei Shonagon in all her humanity. Her crankiness. Her quick intelligence. Her judgmental nature and discerning eye. All her snobbery and human imperfections. That's what makes the work feel so alive, even after all this time. You know, you do all this spiritual practice, and in the end, you come to this appreciation of people being just who they are. That's a very Zen thing. A very Zen way to be.

Ruth Ozeki is a novelist, filmmaker, and Zen Buddhist priest. Her first two novels, My Year of Meats *and* All Over Creation, *have been translated into eleven languages and published in fourteen countries. Her most recent work,* A Tale for the Time Being, *won a Los Angeles Times Book Prize, was shortlisted for the Man Booker Prize and the National Book Critics' Circle Award, and has been published in more than thirty countries.*

CAROLYN PARKHURST

on *Slaughterhouse-Five*
by Kurt Vonnegut

"Books that knock you off balance"

I've never been much of a sci-fi fan. Most of it seemed kind of odd to me when I was younger. But in high school I read *Slaughterhouse-Five* by Kurt Vonnegut, and it gave me insight into what fiction could be, I guess. I love that it's written in short blurbs, and that there are these repeating themes, and that there's the craziness of putting a sci-fi story in the middle of totally serious things about war. And it has this sort of metafictional aspect, since the narrator is writing a book about his experiences in war.

I loved the idea of taking wildly different story lines and making them come together. I kept track of all the timelines, writing inside the book cover every time he said so-and-so or such-and-such, for example, mentioning the smell of mustard gas. There are all these repeated phrases and motifs. You know, it's crazy—it's a crazy book! I didn't know how to get rid of it, and I didn't really want to get rid of it.

It was the first time I remember doing that kind of literary analysis or deconstruction on my own, for my own pleasure and purpose, although I was certainly doing so with the kind of academic tone that I knew from school. It kind of started with me looking at the book and taking it apart, seeing how he wrote it and how he put things together. Looking at it from a more writerly perspective instead of a readerly one.

I pretty much always wanted to be a writer, from first grade on, but I didn't usually approach books as a Future Writer. The only link in my mind, for years, between writing and reading was that I loved reading. That made me want to be a writer, because I loved the experience of sitting down with a great book. I hoped I could do something similar.

So to explain how I got to *Slaughterhouse-Five* and thinking like a writer: When I was younger, I had a book called *Jellybeans for Breakfast* that is about some little girls thinking up new ways to play. "Come to my house and we'll play school. You can be the student—and you can be bad. Come to my house and we'll play house. I'll be the mom, and I'll serve jellybeans for breakfast." That sort of thing.

I remember it as the first time I knew the imagination had no limits. Once I mentioned the book to a friend and she said, "You can't eat jellybeans for breakfast!" And I just thought: "Okay, I'm not going to share this book with you." That's not what it's about. It's about that you can do anything. You can make up a world and start from scratch and put any characters and events and details you want into it, and see what happens.

That's what *Slaughterhouse-Five* meant to me when I encountered it. You can do anything. There aren't any rules. People in writing programs love to say things like "You should never write a book in the second person. You should never write an unsympathetic character." I don't buy any of that.

Vonnegut's radical reshaping of narrative showed me that I wasn't alone, that I didn't have to buy into any rules. You're not supposed to speak directly to a hypothetical reader who's doing the same thing as you're doing right now! But he does it, and he makes it work. I like books that knock you off balance. I like unreliable narrators who think differently. When I was writing *The Dogs of Babel*, I wasn't thinking, "It's going to take a lot for people to believe that this guy is sitting here and he's trying to make this dog talk." So I put in all of these historical examples of people making dogs talk.

That was all totally made up. The idea is to make people wonder: "What world are we in here? What are the rules of this world?"

Carolyn Parkhurst wrote The Dogs of Babel, *a* New York Times *bestseller and a* New York Times *Notable Book. Her next novels were* Lost and Found *and* The Nobodies Album, *as well as the children's book* Cooking with Henry and Elliebelly, *illustrated by Dan Yaccarino. She lives in Washington, DC, with her husband and two children.*

RICHARD PEABODY

on *At Swim-Two-Birds*
by Flann O'Brien

"A ray of light"

I read a ton as a kid, lots of science fiction, and once I found Huxley, lots of experimental stuff, too. But even though I was reading great stuff, I was reading without discernment—which is totally fine, but once I did read something that struck me, I realized that reading with discernment can be so much more.

The way we were taught when I went to school was that if a writer wasn't British, he wasn't any good. And yes, "he," because the way we were taught, there weren't any "she" writers! I had so little awareness of American writers. So little. You may not believe this, but I didn't know there were any living writers until I read a *Washington Post* article on James Grady, which is when *Six Days of the Condor* was being made into a film called *Three Days of the Condor*. I said to myself, "My God, there's a living author. And he lives here, in DC!"

I had no idea writers were living, that writers could make

a living (now, that's funny—but that's a different conversation). There were no TV shows where authors appeared. So I get to this Irish literature class in graduate school and I don't know anything about Irish literature at all. We read a few books, and suddenly, there's *At Swim-Two-Birds* by Flann O'Brien, and it blew my mind.

"This is what I want to do," I thought. "I'm not going to sit around analyzing literature. I'm going to write it." I tried transferring into the creative writing program then, but the teacher rejected me, told me my writing was pedestrian. "I'll show you," I thought. That's all I needed.

So, the start of *Gargoyle* was me and two guys who couldn't get published. No one would print our stuff, so we decided to print it ourselves. When we put the word out that we were publishing a literary magazine, we found ourselves buried in submissions that were so much better than anything the three of us were writing. It was a real wake-up call, and a good one. Now I'm leery of any journal where the editors publish their own work.

The irony is that O'Brien made me want to write—and wanting to write made me want to support writers other than myself. There is so much harsh, hard talk in the book world. Once I paid to go to a conference, and in the novel workshop Larry McMurtry told us, "Most of the people in this room should probably just take up basket weaving." Jack Shoemaker once said at an F. Scott Fitzgerald conference that his house has only taken two things over the transom—"Otherwise, you guys could do something else, because the odds in this business are terrible."

Hearing things like that frustrates me, because I like to give people a chance. There's so few reasons to keep writing other than to share your work and maybe see a little of it in print. At this point, I've amassed so many pages that I've published. It does seem to be that if you do something long enough, you get attention! It's like what Sonny Rollins, the jazz musician, said when someone asked, "How come you have all these records?" He responded, "Well, I've played longer than anyone else." As long as you're still playing, you have the chance to still share and produce.

Sometimes I think that words and publishing and stories matter more in other places, like Ireland. *At Swim-Two-Birds*, to me, was a ray of light, something that shone true in the middle of all the lesser stuff I'd been fed in school and college. Some people find dozens of books like that much earlier. Some people never find a book like that. I feel lucky that I discovered Flann O'Brien exactly when I did, because that novel really did change my life. Even if I hadn't decided to write, hadn't decided to publish, hadn't decided to teach writing, it would have opened me up to a new way of seeing and hearing and experiencing.

Richard Peabody is a poet, editor, and publisher based in Washington, DC. A cofounder of the literary magazine Gargoyle, *he began Paycock Press in 1976 to publish that journal and has since edited half a dozen anthologies of work by women writers.*

Nancy Pearl

on *A Gay and Melancholy Sound*
by Merle Miller

"The kind of pain somebody else could be in"

A lot of books that I read as a teenager—and lots of books that were available then—gave me a view of life that perhaps wasn't the best, most helpful view for growing up in the world in which we live. I loved them at the time. I'm talking about books that I guess we could call "soda-shop books," by authors like Betty Cavanaugh, Anne Emery, even Beverly Cleary's teen novels like *Jean and Johnny*. There was a boy next door, and you both liked each other, but then he starts dating someone else . . . Those are the "big problems." I think that made me feel that that was the ideal of life, you know? Like your mother was this wonderful seamstress and she could make you prom dresses and your sister's prom dress would be the same style but in a different color. It was a very un-realistic world portrayed and I was at an impressionable age.

Those books did keep me reading, and reading led me to my career as a librarian. But it wasn't until 1970 that a book showed me the kind of pain somebody else could be in. *A Gay and Melancholy Sound* by Merle Miller was a somewhat autobiographical novel about a young man growing up in Iowa, in a difficult family, attempting to come to terms with who he is, which happens to be homosexual.

This book had been published in the early 1960s. It wasn't the time that you could admit that to anybody, especially in the Midwest. The narrator is in the process of recording his life on reel-to-reel tapes and trying to decide whether he wants to live or not. And if he doesn't want to live, how he's going to kill himself, and do it with the least harm to anybody that he cares about.

He feels he's failed everybody in his life. There's a scene where he does something as a young man that is really unspeakably cruel, emotionally cruel, to somebody else. Reading this book and seeing the tragedy of this man's life play out showed me what real self-hatred was. It gave me a picture of the kind of pain that somebody could be in that I wasn't. I had a difficult adolescence and I was certainly not happy in college, but it was nothing compared to the extent that Miller showed one could hurt and be hurt. It was kind of a lesson, a lesson in how not to be, written in such beautiful prose that you want to underline every sentence. It's an amazing book.

I fell in love with Miller's books and read as many as I could find. But no one has ever heard of him! Once my husband and I were driving through Iowa and we came upon Marshalltown, where Miller grew up. I said, "Oh, we have to stop! There's a bookstore there. They will have Miller's new novel even though nobody else has it." We go inside and ask, "Do you have the new Merle Miller?" "Oh yes," says the owner, "it's in the window." I didn't see them, so I went outside—and the books in the window were by Henry Miller. Even in his own hometown this author was unknown.

Fortunately, Merle Miller didn't remain in that hometown, even psychically. After Stonewall happened, he chose to come out as a gay man on *The Dick Cavett Show*. He wrote an article for the *New York Times Magazine* that was, for many years, its most-read piece.

What *A Gay and Melancholy Sound* did for me was to galvanize my wish to communicate to readers why a book might be important for them. I wanted to say, "Here's a book that will help you with . . . ," and "I love this book and maybe you will, too, because . . ." It made me realize that not every book is for every reader, and to work hard to help people find the books that would speak to them. Everybody reads a different version of the same book, just as we bring ourselves to every book we read. I believe we don't recognize enough the reasons that we love the books we love, what it is that they fulfill for us.

Nancy Pearl, author of the Book Lust *series and the model for the Librarian Action Figure, is a rock star among readers. The former executive director of the Washington Center for the Book, lifelong librarian, and tastemaker, Pearl developed the One City, One Book program.*

JODI PICOULT

on *Gone with the Wind*
by Margaret Mitchell

"The whole reason that we have art in the world"

I was completely captivated by *Gone with the Wind* when I was thirteen. So captivated that I would act out scenes where I played both Rhett and Scarlett. This is why I didn't actually have a boyfriend until I was fifteen years old!

I went to the library every week with my mom, which might be another reason my romantic life got off to a late start. But my mother probably pointed me toward *Gone with the Wind*, and I was completely blown away by how Margaret Mitchell had created an entire world out of words. It's the first time I remember thinking, "Well, maybe I can do that." Another thing, back to that late-blooming dating scene: *Gone with the Wind* is the perfect romance for a thirteen-year-old. I had never actually done anything with boys beyond talking to them at school. And Rhett and Scarlett have this cat-and-mouse game of a love that there's nothing really sexual about, nothing that would have upset the apple cart of my innocence.

But the reason it's the book that has changed my life has to do with rereading it. When I was thirteen, it was all about grand, sweeping, star-crossed romance. At forty-nine, I feel very, very differently about it. I grew up in a very white community, not thinking a lot about issues of race and social justice, because I didn't have to.

Now that I am more aware of those issues, and I see my role in them as a white person, that's what I see when I read the novel again. I see the way people of color are portrayed. I see that they are caricatures compared to the richer, white characters. And I recognize it as a snapshot of history, a snapshot taken through a 1930s lens.

Margaret Mitchell is a product of her own society. I guess that's the best way to put it. And it's important, I think, for us as readers to recognize it as just that, as a snapshot of what the world was for a certain group of people. But it's also our responsibility as readers to open up our minds to critical thinking and to ask, "What do I feel about that, why do I feel it?" and to acknowledge that what Mitchell represented in her book is not necessarily an accurate portrait. To me the whole point of going back to a book like *Gone with the Wind* is to recognize your responsibility and your clarity of vision from the future looking back. And that's what makes it important. That's what makes fiction important.

A lot of white people nowadays may not be willing to talk about racism because it's uncomfortable. It makes us feel itchy. We have the privilege to not talk about it because we're white. Maybe what you can do is read a book like this instead where it's "fiction"—and I say that in quotes because I mean it with sarcasm—and you can begin to talk about racism and about people of color through that security blanket.

What Mitchell left out, of course, was the fact that the South would not have had its glory if it had not been built on the backs of people of color who never asked to be here. And that to me is really upsetting on a personal level. When I look at *Gone with the Wind*, it's my way of addressing that, of acknowledging it, of recognizing it, and of seeing the flaw in that fiction.

I don't necessarily believe that Margaret Mitchell was doing an intentional thing in portraying people of color the way she did. On the other hand, for me it's very intentional when I write. When I address a topic, I'm doing it specifically because I know it's hard for people to talk about in reality. So let's let them start talking about it through fiction, and then they wind up thinking about their own thoughts and opinions on a very contentious issue in the real world because you've opened their minds up to it.

I would like to believe that if Margaret Mitchell were here today, she would recognize that about her own book. I believe that that's the purpose of fiction, that it allows you to address topics that are difficult by putting a human face on a tough topic. Harvey Milk said, come out, and show people who you are. Show them that they don't have to be afraid of you. Fiction gets people to think about things in a way that opens their minds. If there's anything that can make you do that, whether it's a book or a movie or a conversation or a personal experience, that's what makes us grow as people. And for me that's the whole reason that we have art in the world.

Jodi Picoult is the bestselling author of twenty-three novels. Her books are translated into thirty-four languages in thirty-five countries.

Gerald Richards

on *The Autobiography of Malcolm X*

"The importance of that context to us right now"

My sister gave me *The Autobiography of Malcolm X* when I was sixteen or seventeen. I grew up in Harlem, and our family was lower-class, but we always had books. My sister was and still is an avid reader, and she gave me that book at a particularly potent time in my life.

I won a scholarship to private school, so I wound up one of five African American kids in an all-white prep school in Manhattan. I think my sister gave me the book when she did because she thought I needed a little more blackness in my life at a time when my schoolwork was centered on Shakespeare and all of the other white literary figures in the traditional canon.

Growing up, I heard much more about Martin Luther King Jr. than I did about Malcolm X. I knew about Malcolm, but not much. Getting a book that was a lot about black identity, about a man growing up and finding out where he belonged, was important to me then, because I was trying to figure the same things out for myself. Here comes a book that is all about being African American. It's all about blackness. It's all about defining yourself as a young black man, understanding your past, and discerning your personal mission.

College wasn't a given in my working-class family; the sister who gave me that book, for instance, never went to college. I won't say I was lucky to get the scholarships that I did. I'll say those scholarships were fortuitous. I wound up going to Wesleyan University. How do you find the path to your identity, because you're going to college and you're supposed to "find yourself" there? How do you center yourself and not forget where you come from? You're on your own for the first time, really, when you get to college—for many of us, if not all of us.

Wesleyan may be just a couple of hours from New York City, but it's far. It's miles and miles away, culturally and psychically, from where I grew up and how I was raised. At the time I was there, the African American population was maybe 10 percent of the school. At least I was going from a private school to a prestigious college; some people, who came straight from inner-city public schools, can drown when they get to an elite college. They don't have support, or connections, or the tools they need. They leave because it's so hard.

But I walked in with great family support, a strong education— and a very strong sense of who I was and who I wanted to be.

And who I didn't want to be. I'm in no way, shape, or form a militant. Malcolm X is hard-core. He was a soldier, and he was fighting. There were parts of his story I couldn't connect to, and I wondered, when I read them, if I had to be antiwhite in order to fit in. But I kept reading, and the important thing is that by the end of the book, he changed. He had come around to understanding the power of working together.

Talking about *The Autobiography of Malcolm X* is making me

want to go out and buy it and read it again. Reading it, being seen reading it—these things were rites of passage for young African American students in the 1980s. "You have to read this book," people would tell each other. I remember wondering what other people were getting out of it. And I never actually went back to my sister and asked her what she got out of it. We're much closer now, but at the time we had kind of split paths.

Malcolm's book isn't just about his personal history. It tells us a lot about American history. I'm amazed, really, that this book isn't taught in every school to everyone, given its historical context and the importance of that context to us right now, today.

How many young men and women are giving *The Autobiography of Malcolm X* to sisters and brothers now? I'd love to know. I live in a very white world. I'm an African American man. Which way do you go? Down the path of the savior, like King? Or the militant, like Malcolm?

Gerald Richards is the chief executive officer of 826 National. He has a BA in film studies from Wesleyan University and an MFA in writing from the School of the Art Institute of Chicago.

MELISSA RIVERS

on *The Story of Ferdinand*
by Munro Leaf

"Such a subversive story"

My mom read *The Story of Ferdinand* to me as a child, and I have read it to my son, and then my mom read it to my son's preschool class. I have an old copy, from when it was first published in the 1940s, and it's such a subversive story: it's okay to be different, it's okay to be you, it's okay not to cave in to peer pressure. At the time *Ferdinand* was written, that was not a message that was given to people.

It's a charming story, on the surface, but when you really step back and hear its message, you realize that it's a huge one for such a small, sweet book. Leaf was telling children that you don't have to be bullied because of who you are, even if you're a big, strong . . . bull. It's okay to like sweet things, little things. It's such a simple story, but it has all these values. You don't even really get the message until you're a parent yourself.

Today, I am not only an avid reader, I'm a voracious reader.

It took me a while to find the things I really loved, but toward the end of high school, I did, and I wound up as a history major in college. I am never, ever without a book, and although I know I'm missing out on some great stuff, I really only read nonfiction. I get that from my parents. Life is so fascinating that no matter what you can make up, what's already happened is even crazier.

I love true crime, but I also go on these weird topical phases—a Teddy Roosevelt phase, a Custer phase—and those things sometimes kick me in different directions, too. Right now I'm reading a lot of eighteenth-century history, but almost working backward, from Queen Mary to George III and probably George II after that. Believe it or not, I love Bill O'Reilly's books, and I just want to say to my son's teachers—he's fourteen now—reading this kind of stuff is how you get your students to learn!

My dad loved history, especially about World War II, as his family had escaped from Germany. My mom loved anything to do with seventeenth-century France and England, especially concerning the courts. I still read with my son and encourage him to read, too, although like with most teenagers it can be like pulling teeth. He loved *The Catcher in the Rye* but didn't care for *To Kill a Mockingbird*. However, I'm encouraged by the fact that he didn't mind Shakespeare. I guess I have to remember the lessons of the book we started out talking about, that it's okay for him to be himself. But I'll be here to remind him he comes from a family of readers.

Melissa Rivers is an actor, TV host and producer, and philanthropist. She is the daughter of the late comedian Joan Rivers and the late producer Edgar Rosenberg. She wrote The Book of Joan: Tales of Mirth, Mischief, and Manipulation, *about life with her iconic mother.*

AL ROKER

on *The Adventures of Sherlock Holmes*
by Sir Arthur Conan Doyle

"Being able to figure things out"

The first book I remember is *Green Eggs and Ham;* my parents must have read it to me hundreds of times. And what I remember that is so funny is in my mind the book is wildly colorful, almost psychedelic—but the actual book has, what? Three colors? Maybe four, if you count the inky black outlines on the figures. It charged my imagination up so much that in my head it was like a Peter Max painting or something.

That's one of the anecdotal reasons I think reading to children is so important. I know there are a lot of studies about this now, and I couldn't possibly tell you any facts about them at this moment, but my own memories of being read to and reading to my children have shown me that something powerful happens when you combine love and time and imagination.

So maybe *Green Eggs and Ham* should be the book that changed my life, but the book that I was old enough to believe changed my life was definitely my first collection of Sherlock Holmes stories. Sure, sure, I was a shy, awkward kid who wasn't particularly athletic, and that's why I found a refuge in reading, but you can hear that from lots of people. What was so meaningful to me in Sir Arthur Conan Doyle's work was the idea of being able to figure things out, and that's huge to shy, awkward kids for whom life isn't easily figured out.

Sherlock Holmes didn't care what anyone else did, what anyone else looked like, or what anyone else wore. He put on his deerstalker cap and cape, or he picked up his violin for a while, or he sat and smoked and ignored the other people in the room. He just did his own thing in his own time, and everybody thought he was the most amazing person ever. To tell you the truth, that might have been interesting enough. But then he proves he's the most amazing person ever by figuring things out from the smallest clues possible. I digress, but I have to say that that's fascinating to me now as a meteorologist, because we have to look for those small clues, yet even when we find them they aren't always accurate. Don't blame the weatherman!

Back to Holmes. Reading these mysteries made me feel as if I were in on something, both a kind of secret, a way of reading the world, and also a club, people who loved Sherlock Holmes and Dr. Watson and wanted to learn more about their methods. You can read these stories again and again and never be bored, which is saying something, especially for the adolescent boys who were the Holmes fans when I was growing up.

I do go back to Holmes from time to time, although my own son isn't as fascinated by the stories as I was—and that's perfectly okay. Another kid might not have loved *Green Eggs and Ham* the way I did. Reading is important, but it's also highly individual. You have to help your children find the books, the stories, that they connect to most strongly, and not just foist your favorites on them.

Al Roker is a television personality, a weatherman for NBC's Today show, *and a nine-time Emmy winner. His latest book,* Storm of the Century: Tragedy, Heroism, Survival, and the Epic True Story of America's Deadliest Natural Disaster: The Great Gulf Hurricane of 1900, *came out in 2015.*

RICHARD RUSSO

on *Pudd'nhead Wilson*
by Mark Twain

"A very human concept of optimism"

For a writer, a book can change your life, and a book can also be the
one that helped you most become the writer that you are. Maybe
that's the same thing. And for me, [the writer of that book] was
Mark Twain, perhaps because I'd been reading and studying him
long before it ever occurred to me that I wanted to be a writer.

So I read him in high school, then I read him again in college,
and then again in graduate school, and finally, when I was almost
finished with my PhD, realized how much I'd been influenced by
him. I also realized how quintessentially American a writer he
was, which helped me to grasp the kind of writer that I was and
wanted to be. And there was nobody more important than Twain
because his work showed me that in order to go to the really dark
places that I wanted to, if I was going to go into the world that
Twain entered, a world of poverty and ignorance and racism and
violence, that I had better go armed with humor.

People simply weren't going to follow me there unless I was going to entertain them first. Most of my studies in college and graduate school kind of had it the other way around. And it was Twain that made me understand that no, first you get people to laugh, and if you can do that, maybe, just maybe, at the end, you have some instruction. Twain gave me permission to be funny, to have a comic sense of the world, and to experiment not just with story, but with a very human concept of optimism.

Pudd'nhead Wilson is very much a product of its time, when race was a big American problem. Race is still a big American problem, and the premise in Twain's novel shows how much we fear the concept of blackness: when one drop, just "one drop" of "black" blood, determines your defined race, that's a terrifying time to negotiate. But the book is just so damn funny that it takes fears and turns them into something more, something exaggerated that shows these fears as the illogical thoughts of idiots.

Twain is one of the really funny writers who sometimes goes down that road where you can kind of discern where the world isn't fun anymore. His secret is that the humor comes at a price, and he knows this.

To completely understand *Pudd'nhead Wilson*, though, took me until I taught Twain's last novel, *The Mysterious Stranger*, which has a noticeable absence of hope. At that point, Twain had lost his beloved wife. Would I be the same writer I am now if I'd lost a wife, a child? I'd guess not.

So here's the thing. *Pudd'nhead Wilson* is, as much as I love the novel, very much a period piece. You can't escape that. Despite the fact that Twain obviously had great affection for people of color, he calls them "the Negro race." But it's much, much worse than that. You teach this book, you can see that it's a period piece, you can see that it's part of a different time in our country, and you can see that so little has changed. God, you feel so stupid. The book's trajectory is from a kind of protected innocence to a type of knowledge and wisdom. But where are we now? Did *anybody* read *Huckleberry Finn*?

Twain's novels still have resonance. Perhaps mostly for white readers. I think black readers may not get the same solace from books like *To Kill a Mockingbird* as white readers do. For not seeing it the same way, with the same enthusiasm and fervor.

My teaching of Twain, I now realize, had to accommodate a certain evolution of my own, from my state as a younger writer and reader who glimpsed a kind of revelation in *Pudd'nhead Wilson*, to an older writer and reader who, in the twenty-first century, understands that humor can be condiment instead of main course.

Richard Russo is the acclaimed, bestselling author of Empire Falls, Bridge of Sighs, *and* Nobody's Fool, *among others. His memoir,* Elsewhere, *examined how his mother's mental illness affected his small-town, blue-collar upbringing.*

SAÏD SAYRAFIEZADEH

on *Krapp's Last Tape*
by Samuel Beckett

"Something inside of me shifted"

Nineteen ninety-two. I was twenty-three, in Pittsburgh, and I was an actor. I was performing in an evening of Beckett plays; I was in two of them. The final show of the night was *Krapp's Last Tape*.

It was performed by a thirty-nine-year-old actor who ran the theater company. I remember that when we first did a read-through of all the plays, that one seemed impenetrable. I didn't understand it. It's filled with stage directions, and the actor read them all aloud. It's boring and confusing. I didn't get it.

And then, four weeks later, I was finally able to watch him in the final dress. It was a very small, run-down theater, and I went out and sat in the audience and that play just devastated me.

The play, you know, it's about this man reflecting back on his life. The thirty-nine-year-old actor was made up to look as if he were sixty-nine. The character is listening to a recording of himself that he made on his thirty-ninth birthday, which made it so meta. At thirty-nine, the character had had all of these aspirations. He's still, at sixty-nine, a bit full of himself, and of course the audience sees all of these layers, sees that what he was imagining his life to be did not come to pass.

I was twenty-three and I wanted to be an actor and a writer. I wanted to leave Pittsburgh, but I felt stuck there. I wanted to move to New York and give it a shot, but it was terrifying. Pittsburgh was very comforting. I'd grown up there.

When I saw that play—I don't think this is me being dramatic—something inside of me shifted. Essentially, Beckett is saying time passes, and you can't have it all. I may have been the only person sitting in the audience during that rehearsal, and when I say "the audience," there were probably just about thirty folding chairs, max, set bleacher-style on raised platforms. I felt as if I were alone with the actor. He played the entire thing straight out, sitting at a desk beneath a lone lightbulb.

We had two weeks of performances, and every night, even if I wasn't watching from the audience, I would hear the words of Krapp; I felt like I learned the entire script just by hearing it over and over. The final sentence is the voice from the tape, the thirty-nine-year-old's voice, saying, "Perhaps my best years of happiness are behind me, but I wouldn't want them back, not with the fire in me now." And he has disgust in his voice. And you just see Krapp's vacuous—the Krapp-at-sixty-nine's vacuous stare, and you know what has happened.

That was February 1992. I moved to New York a year later. I didn't pack up that day, but when I look back on it, that was the moment when I made my decision.

I still wanted to be an actor; I'd always wanted to be both an actor and a writer. But the writing came years after. First there were years of struggling and trying to find my way and eventually giving up, but you know, when I finally gave up acting, it actually felt like an accomplishment. Like "Oh good, I don't have to do that anymore." I knew, then, all I was going to do was write.

I knew that if I stayed in Pittsburgh, my art would only ever be a hobby. There is nobody in Pittsburgh making a living as an artist. I overstate, but there were limited opportunities. If it was going to happen, it wasn't going to happen in Pittsburgh. It was going to happen in New York. And it might not happen, but at least I would have tried.

The painful thing, the alternative to moving, would have been staying, and then I would have remained under an illusion of being about to break through, about to make it, on the edge of being big. We said things like that. And we were fooling ourselves. We always thought we were right on the cusp and we weren't. Like Krapp, always on the cusp and never making it. That one night in a dark, empty theater, his voice convinced me to head where things were bright and crowded, and it was the right decision.

Saïd Sayrafiezadeh is the author of the story collection Brief Encounters with the Enemy, *a finalist for the 2014 PEN/Robert W. Bingham Prize, and the critically acclaimed memoir* When Skateboards Will Be Free, *selected as one of the ten best books of the year by Dwight Garner of the* New York Times.

JOHN SCALZI

on *The People's Almanac*
by David Wallechinsky and Irving Wallace

"Nearly everything was understandable"

I first came across it at my grandmother's apartment when I was six years old. It was this big thick book, filled with chapters about all these different subjects, starting with science, moving into pop culture, had a chapter that was all lists, moved on to paranormal stuff . . . And it seemed to me, at six years old, that all the information in the world was in that one book, *The People's Almanac*, and it was amazing to me that there was just so much stuff in there. As a precocious reader I sucked it all in and I learned it so that later on I could just spew it.

It made me really appreciate just how big and interesting the world could be, because there was so much cool stuff in it, and it also inspired my love for finding out about all the cool stuff in the world. It turned me on to trivia books, books about science, books that had as their goal to educate you about the world.

When I was ten, I broke my leg—I was crossing the street and got hit by a car—and I was really worried about what I was going to do laid up in bed. One day my mother appeared with ... *The People's Almanac #2*! I did the same thing—swallowed the whole thing and learned a whole bunch of stuff—and it was fascinating to me.

These books created a baseline of information that I could pull from, as well as a desire to learn more of that information. The other thing that it did, for my fiction as well as my nonfiction, was to create the belief that nearly everything was understandable, as long as you could explain it in terms that anyone could understand. I knew things that grown-ups did not, and that was kind of cool to me. It didn't necessarily mean that I understood what I knew. For example, one section was about sex and sex-related terms. At six years old, I knew the word "clitoris," but I didn't find out what it meant, or was all about, until much, much later.

Of course, I write stories—and what this book gave me was the wide band of knowledge that gives me the ability to trust that I can find the information I need. I don't have to look at things in a very narrow way; it's a sort of multidisciplinary way. Things like robotics and politics all get thrown into the mash. You trust that you can make these things into an interesting story, and since I learned that pretty much anything humans do can be communicated in an accessible way, I learned to believe that anything could go into a story. These little tiny chunks and nuggets grab you and make you interested and make you want to read more. They make the reader want to keep going.

Although kids can now go online for all kinds of information, what a book like *The People's Almanac* has is curation. You can go to Wikipedia—but it's not necessarily browsing friendly, whereas if you have a book containing one hundred facts about the solar system, that is designed to intrigue and to interest and to present information in a very specific way, that's great for people, for readers. We have the dilemma of choice these days. You go into a store and there are fifty blenders to choose from, and you get a paralysis of choice.

When I was six years old, I thought *The People's Almanac* contained the sum of all human knowledge, but now I know it was information that was selected and organized and designed. Books are constrained objects, and within that, you have a wonderful freedom to learn a certain amount that you didn't know you didn't know. You come away from that not knowing everything, but knowing more than you did than when you started.

I have my copies of those books in storage somewhere, because I never throw books away—which is a real problem. Every once in a while, I check to see how much they might cost if I wanted to buy them today. A lot of the info in them is, of course, out-of-date, has been overtaken by events, so what I try to do for my own daughter is buy her books like these, books that show that knowledge is cool and that the more you know, the more you can know. The idea behind my *Almanac*s, that information will open up doors for you? That's never out-of-date.

John Scalzi is an American science fiction writer, online writer, and former president of the Science Fiction and Fantasy Writers of America.

ELISSA SCHAPPELL

on *Nine Stories*
by J. D. Salinger

"We appear in other people's stories"

I grew up in a house where everybody read—it was just what you did. *The Electric Kool-Aid Acid Test, Watership Down, Zen and the Art of Motorcycle Maintenance, The Lord of the Rings, Dune, The Group.* My mother has been in the same book group for over forty years. *Nine Stories* by J. D. Salinger is the first book I remember her selecting especially for me. Making a deal of giving it to me.

My parents were always very equitable, exceedingly so it seems to me at times, and I seem to think that she hadn't also given my sister a special book—only me—and maybe here I'm creating some sort of narrative—perhaps she gave my sister a gold watch or a pony. It felt like she was recognizing the kind of person I was. She knew what I needed. She saw me. And she did, she insists that she had always known I was going to be a writer.

Most important to me, though, was that *Nine Stories* was one of her favorite books. She'd read the stories in college and was, in her words, "totally captivated by them. I wanted to share them with you." Which I wouldn't have imagined. Some years ago she gave me her actual copy, which felt meaningful to me.

So, since my mother gave it to me, I read it.

Honestly, the first time through I was a little confused. The stories disturbed me. The initial story in the collection is "A Perfect Day for Bananafish." I imagined, given the title, that it would be funny. Funny books were my favorite (also books where people exhibited extraordinary gifts like ESP, telekinesis, or the ability to stay alive by eating other human beings) and I fancied myself quite a card. But it wasn't funny ha-ha, it was funny *odd*. It was unnerving. But ultimately unnerving in a way I responded to. As a teenager I loved a surprise ending and stories where desperate people committed shocking acts, which Seymour does, although it wasn't the kind of surprise I was accustomed to, "An Incident at Owl Creek Bridge" shockers. Even so, that story embedded itself in my mind and I never forgot it.

Before *Nine Stories*, most of the short stories I'd read were science fiction, horror, or fairy tales . . . I mostly read novels. I was struck by how little action there was. No one was searching for a lost clock or trying to evade Orc armies, no one was pining on the moors, people were just talking. And drinking. Character was the story and subtext was everything—what wasn't being said or couldn't be said out loud. Growing up in suburban Delaware I completely related to this. I felt at home with these over-sensitive, eccentric characters who smiled and lied and made jokes to keep others at bay, as well as to protect their loved ones from their darkness. They were cracking wise, but they were injured—even the women in "Uncle Wiggly in Connecticut," while they disgusted me, were, I'd later recognize, damaged and full of longing, just trying to solve the problem of being alive.

I recognized those shallow women, and I knew that they were more than what they seemed. I've reread the stories a lot, and when I did so in college, "Uncle Wiggly in Connecticut" resonated because I felt I knew these women, the very model of the preppy social climbers I'd known growing up in Delaware. Wealthy, self-centered, ridiculous, casually racist, and selfish. As I've grown older I've developed more empathy for the characters. These women don't seem silly to me, they seem pathetic, tragic. I've now lived long enough and been in enough relationships that I can relate to their suffering . . . that and their day drinking.

In terms of the stories that featured or referenced a member of the Glass family—Seymour, Boo Boo, Walt—you knew the Glasses, knew how loved they were by each other, and yet, none of them escaped sadness. Being loved doesn't inoculate you against depression or sadness.

But as a teenager I was a little puzzled. I wasn't sure what to think, but without understanding why exactly, I had a deep affection for these stories. What would be clear later on, when I read *Franny and Zooey* and *Raise High the Roofbeams, Carpenter,* was that it was the cosmology—if that is the right word—that Salinger was creating that drew me in. This is what I found so compelling, so comforting.

When I was a junior in high school my father was diagnosed with lymphoma. I was crazy about my father. In some ways he was my center. The idea of him dying was unthinkable to me, even the possibility was unbearable. If he died, I would die.

In Salinger's work people die. Seymour dies. Walt dies. But they are never completely dead, because they are alive at other times in the novels. They are kept alive through the memories the characters share, and the mythologizing that occurs. The act of mythologizing, the ability to see several different sides of character through the prism of other people's perceptions resonated with me. You say crazy, I say philosopher.

Three stories in *Nine Stories* feature characters that appear in the novels. By being able to see characters alive and dead, just mentioned in one story and the star of another, it's like no one really dies. We are connected to these characters in life as well as in death. And the idea of how we appear in other people's stories— we don't die—spoke to my fear of dying and disappearing, and people being lost to us forever.

While the father character in my first book, *Use Me*, isn't exactly my father, there are similarities. So part of writing the book was out of a desire to continue the conversation with him and keep him alive. Every time a reader opens a book, the characters begin to breathe, and ever after we close the book they continue to live in our memory.

It occurs to me that Salinger's choosing to show his characters at different times in their lives and through a variety of different people's lenses speaks to me because I have been a lot of different people in my life, and continue to be. I'm a fiction writer, and a magazine writer, I am an editor and a literary citizen, I am a teacher, a wife and a mother. I am not one person at a fixed time in space, and when I die I hope my books survive me. And, more I hope, if they tell stories about me, they will be good ones, and I won't be gone forever.

Elissa Schappell's collection Use Me *was a runner-up for the 2000 PEN/Hemingway Award. She cofounded* Tin House, *where she is editor at large; she writes* Vanity Fair's *"Hot Type" column. Schappell's latest story collection,* Blueprints for Building Better Girls, *received much critical acclaim. Originally from Delaware, she now lives in Brooklyn with her family.*

LIEV SCHREIBER

on *Anna Karenina*
by Leo Tolstoy

"A real feat of literary magic"

Anna Karenina is the *Citizen Kane* of books, if it were possible to judge or rank literature, if it were an alternate universe where a book could be the number one thing that catches most people.

What's so much fun is the titillating, episodic nature of how Tolstoy chooses to unfold the narrative. What's so remarkable is the description of her death—how he kills her, when he kills her, where he kills her. What happens to the narrative when she dies is a real feat of literary magic. No one has ever brought me closer to understanding death than Tolstoy did in those two or three sentences.

I went to Hampshire College, where you essentially design your own curriculum, so *Anna Karenina* wasn't required reading. My brother made me read it; he told me it was a good book.

There's no good screen adaptation of the novel. Perhaps one day there will be. I think it might be better done through a TV show due to its episodic nature. I can't imagine trying to condense it. It needs to be big. It needs to draw you in.

Another book that had an early and profound effect on me, not a book but a play, was Shakespeare's *King Lear*. I read it in 1987; I was studying acting in England and I started to focus on the character of Edmund, particularly the speech he makes to the goddess of nature, to ask what's different about him, why he doesn't deserve a better life. It was the beginning of a relationship with a writer that I felt connected to and challenged by. There was a very intimate and articulate projection of humanity in Edmund that made this stuff very performable, actable, but it wasn't naturalism. Naturalism wasn't very exciting to me. It was something else, a sort of artifice or heightened state that highlighted what was essential.

One last book I'll mention: When my grandfather died, I had terrific anxiety about being able to remember him, about our memories together, so I started to write a screenplay about a guy who goes to Ukraine to find out where his father is from. Then I read a short story by Jonathan Safran Foer in *The New Yorker* and said, "Holy shit, this is what I've been trying to do!" When *Everything Is Illuminated* came out I thought it was really beautiful. When I directed the film, I greatly diminished Jonathan's novel, but fortunately he feels that the novel is the novel, and anything that comes after it or out of it is its own thing.

Liev Schreiber is an actor, screenwriter, and director who lives in New York City. He received a Golden Globe nomination in 2014 for his role as Ray Donovan on television.

JIM SHEPARD

on the collected works of J. D. Salinger

"We're talking about fallible beings here"

Someone gave me the collected works of J. D. Salinger—you remember, the paperbacks in the box, the ones where the covers were just one color with the title? That seemed particularly perverse and joyless, not having an image on the cover. I mean, if it's just a red cover that says *The Catcher in the Rye*? Normally that would have made it much easier for me to ignore it. I couldn't figure out what they might be about, what kind of books these were, and so, perversely, I cracked one open and started reading.

I was probably ten or fifteen pages in and thinking, "When on earth is this going to turn into what I recognize as literary stuff?" But it just kept being guys sitting around saying things like "Did you eat yet?" "No, did you?" And I just thought this was hilarious. It sounded like the kind of horseshit that went on in my own family; how could this be important writing? The fact that I was both not bored and that I felt like I was starting to learn about the characters kept me going. The writing was so aggressively willing to have at this subject, to wrestle with finality, to watch people wrestling with finality. It all seemed quite revelatory to me in a wonderful way.

On that rainy Saturday—I must have been eleven or twelve at the time—I finished two of the books in that slipcase, swallowed them whole. The idea that a writer could create this world! I'd sort of seen a version of that, read a few things like H. P. Lovecraft, but I hadn't seen it done with Salinger's kind of naturalism. To me, making up a world and its characters out of whole cloth was something you did in fantasy.

Salinger repays rereading, but I don't revisit him regularly, both because I have taught his work at various points and because I think in some ways he's more effective for young people because he's focused on issues that they care about. In some ways, his young people exist in a more innocent time, too, and I have become more interested in looking at innocence from a different angle. Sometimes in my own work I handle something that seems quite subversive or critical—but there's an enormous amount of generosity underlying it; at least that's what I'm trying do.

I write a lot about man-made catastrophes, which means there's a lot of criticism implicit in my choice of subject. Who is it that allowed us to get to this state? That kind of thing. But I'm always conscious of the humanity underneath. At the end of my most recent novel, *The Book of Aron*, there's a line about having the right to make mistakes. We have the responsibility to register that we have made mistakes, and to try to do the best we can not to make them again. And, of course, I'm fascinated and appalled by the ways we pretend that we haven't made mistakes.

I am aware—and I try to remain so—that we're talking about fallible beings here. If you feel like you're reading something that's being created by someone who doesn't in some way love his characters, it seems very misanthropic. Because, you understand, the author is the person putting these characters through this kind of suffering. If you don't love your characters, it feels like you're pulling the wings off flies.

Salinger, even though he deals with adolescent concerns, has that generosity of spirit. He's ferocious on people he thinks are "phonies" (of course, that's Holden Caulfield's word, not his), but he also has such tenderness toward those people who are doing the best they can and just muddling along.

Jim Shepard's latest novel is The Book of Aron. *His six previous novels and four short-story collections include the National Book Award nominee* Like You'd Understand, Anyway *and* You Think That's Bad. *He teaches creative writing at Williams College.*

REBECCA SKLOOT

on *Literary Journalism*
edited by Norman Sims and Mark Kramer

"That was everything"

I had no interest in becoming a writer—from the time I was
about four years old, I was sure I'd become a veterinarian, so
I went through most of schooling with what I now refer to as
"veterinary tunnel vision." I thought any non-science class was
a waste of my time, because it wouldn't help me become a vet,
so I only took classes like biochemistry, biostatistics, neuroanat-
omy, and histology. About as nonliterary as you can get. I took
five years off between high school and college, so by the time I
got there I was older than most of my classmates, and felt like I
didn't have time to take electives. I signed up for my first writing course late in my junior year because, for some reason, my
school counted creative writing as a foreign language, which was
required to graduate. I figured a writing class that met once a
week would take less time away from my science classes than a
foreign language class that met five times a week (for the record,

I really wish I spoke a foreign language now, but I'm very glad I took the writing class instead).

One of my first writing assignments was, "Write a story about something someone forgot." I scribbled, "Henrietta Lacks" at the top of my page, then wrote about the fact that the whole world seemed to have forgotten about her, but I couldn't. I was weirdly obsessed with her. Henrietta's amazing immortal cells were one of the most important things that happened to science, yet no one knew anything about her, except that she was black. I'd been obsessed with her since I learned of her at sixteen.

I loved that class—I wrote story after story, all of them somehow related to science. My teacher, John Calderazzo, realized I was a writer long before I did, but he didn't push it at first. He just gave me a book: *Literary Journalism*, edited by Norman Sims and Mark Kramer. I read its introduction, "The Art of Literary Journalism," and freaked out. It talked of immersing yourself in people's lives, of the need to "bear witness" to important stories. I called my father, who is also a writer, and told him how excited I was about this class, this book. A few days later, a second book, *The New Science Journalists*, showed up in my mailbox with a note from my father: *These are your people*, he wrote. *You can do this.* That book, edited by Ted Anton and Rick McCourt, collected writing by "literary science journalists," writers who didn't just report the dry facts of science, but who wrote gripping stories that brought science to life.

These books introduced me to a world of writing that combines creativity with reporting to produce stories that read like fiction, but are journalistically accurate and true. This included Susan Orlean's amazing profile, "The American Man, at Age Ten," an essay from what would become Adrian Nicole LeBlanc's incredible book, *Random Family*, Deborah Blum on the battles between primate researchers and animal rights activists, and many others—people who became role models, and fortunately, in some cases, friends. But the one story I read more than any other was Ted Conover's "Trucking Through the AIDS Belt," which uses the narrative of a road trip to tell an essential story about global health. I read that thing over and over, underlining and highlighting, amazed by the tremendous risks he took as a reporter that let him manifest fears in his readers. His was the kind of tension you can only write by putting yourself in the middle of a story. I realized, "Oh, that's how you do it. That's how you really understand a story: You go in the middle of it and you live there and you take risks, even if people think you're crazy and try to stop you."

I pulled out my original copy of *Literary Journalism* before this interview and it's amazing to look at all these years later: The sentences I underlined, the notes I made in the margins; I had no idea, but that was me outlining my future philosophy as a writer, mapping out my adult life. I laughed when I turned to the final page of Norman Sims's introduction: There, in red ink, underlined for emphasis, I wrote, "Love it. See me doing it."

My father and John both realized early on that I was interested in doing a unique kind of science writing, but I still thought I was going to become a veterinarian. I just thought maybe I'd write as a hobby. Eventually John gave me a stack of catalogues for graduate creative writing programs, and said, "You know, you don't have to become a vet just because that's what you always thought you'd do." He made the case for why he thought I actually wanted to become a science writer, not a vet. Then he said something I've now repeated to many, many students. He said, "Letting go of a goal doesn't mean you failed, as long as you have a new goal in its place. That's not giving up; it's just changing directions, which can be one of the most important things you can do in your life." He was right.

Almost twenty years later, when I finished writing *The Immortal Life of Henrietta Lacks*, I got e-mails from Ted Conover, Adrian Nicole LeBlanc, Susan Orlean, and Deborah Blum basically saying: *You did it, kid*—that was everything.

Rebecca Skloot is the author of the New York Times *bestseller* The Immortal Life of Henrietta Lacks. *Her award-winning science writing has appeared in the* New York Times Magazine, O, The Oprah Magazine, Discover, *and many other publications.*

KARIN SLAUGHTER

on *Mystery and Manners*
by Flannery O'Connor

"To read these stories was a revelation"

Growing up in the South, there's this long history of writing, some of it quite problematic, so when I was thinking about which book truly affected my life, I decided to bypass *Gone with the Wind* and that kind of thing. I'm choosing a book by a truly great Southern writer, but it's not a book that deals with the flaws of the South, at least not in the same way. I'm choosing *Mystery and Manners* by Flannery O'Connor.

I think it's bullshit when writers say they don't write about where they're from. Even if you read Ray Bradbury, he's really writing about his hometown. When I first started reading O'Connor's stories, I loved them. They were grotesque and violent and kind of crazy, and I was amazed—one, that a woman could write about that stuff; they were very unladylike. I grew up with every adult in my life telling me every five minutes to cross my legs. To read these stories was a revelation.

When I got older and read *Mystery and Manners*, it was a real lightbulb moment. One of my favorite moments is when someone asks her if writing programs "stifle writers," and O'Connor says, "I think they don't stifle them enough." Which I just think is great, since now most of them are just ATM machines . . .

The way she used religion, the way she used character—she was really talking about a different story than the one you were reading. So you could read one of her stories as a young person and think, "Isn't this crazy and hilarious about the prosthetic leg?" and then read it again later and realize it's really about isolation, and entrapment, and the way women are treated. How devastating the financial situation of certain people is throughout their lives. When you read "A Good Man Is Hard to Find" as an adult, you read a line like "She would have been a good woman if there'd been somebody there to kill her every day of her life," and you wonder, who is worse? The misfit or the grandmother? She's a hypocrite who can't accept who he is. He knows who he is. He's not good. But he knows it.

I write pretty graphic crime novels. What O'Connor did so well is that whether her characters are good people or bad people, you understood them. I think that's an important lesson for any crime writer. I don't like books where someone does something just because they're bad. Being bad is a choice. Most criminals end up in prison through a series of bad choices, like a series of Russian nesting dolls. There's something asinine they did, and then they make bad choices to cover it up. That's not "I'm being my own man," that's just being stupid!

She really believed that we have agency. She grew up in a small Southern town, she was very unusual—her claim to fame is that she taught a chicken to walk backward. That's the kind of stupid thing I would have done as a kid, by the way. But she managed to modify the crazy thoughts in her head into something that was universal.

For example, if I went to my high school classmates now and asked them what high school was like for them, they would say, "It was hell." High school isn't the best time of anybody's life. All right, sadly, for some people, it is. But for most of us, and not just the writers and the Flannery O'Connors and the Karin Slaughters of the world, it's not fun. Everybody thinks she's an outsider. O'Connor used that perspective.

At a point when she could have gone on, she became sick and had to move home and live with her mother. She had had this glimpse of a different life, of a life in New York City, a life where she could have had great worldwide success, and she had that taken away from her. That's so sad, but she used that, too.

Karin Slaughter is the internationally bestselling author of several novels, including the Grant County *series. A longtime resident of Atlanta, she splits her time between the kitchen and the living room.*

ANDREW SOLOMON

on *Rootabaga Stories*
by Carl Sandburg

"A tolerance for what's strange or different"

Carl Sandburg wrote *Rootabaga Stories* because he thought fairy tales set among princes and princesses in castles lacked an American idiom. He wanted to write fantastical stories for Americans, full of popcorn and railroads, and the stories that resulted are lyrical, exuberant, and a little bit melancholy. In them, no boundaries exist between possibility and impossibility.

My father read them to me, when I was six or seven, and I remember how much I loved Sandburg's use of melodic and strange and complex prose poetry. The stories are deeply, richly, and fantastically imagined. My sense of language just exploded. I love words, and now that I'm a father and see how much my son loves words, too, I wonder if that's what I was like at the same age.

For me, writing is an act of freedom, and *Rootabaga Stories* appealed to my sense of ingenuity and wildness. Even today, when I'm writing serious nonfiction books, I believe my imagination should not be constrained by literalism. Things should be accurate, but not necessarily literal. It's a relief to escape into allusion and measured obliquity, to free myself from the rigors of nuance-free reporting.

When I reread Sandburg's stories to my son, his tropes leap out at me, almost as if my memory were a pop-up book. My favorite story is "How Six Pigeons Came Back to Hatrack the Horse After Many Accidents and Six Telegrams." George has heard it dozens of times. A few years ago, a new acquaintance had come for tea and we started talking about the book. I went upstairs, retrieved my copy, and read "Six Pigeons" out loud to her. We've been great friends ever since. Likewise, I read the stories on my own, so often that the book has a permanent place on my bedside table.

I didn't know what empathy was until I was much older, and I learned a lot about it from other books, such as the novels of Virginia Woolf. Woolf, Tolstoy, Proust, and George Eliot—all of whom I studied and about all of whom I have written. But some of the origins of that lay in Sandburg's stories, which have a very specific kindness in them, a generosity of spirit in their feats of invention. *Rootabaga Stories* helped me learn to listen. You couldn't know what was next, so you had to simply pay attention. What followed might not make sense to you at first, but if you kept listening, it would. Reading these books taught me how to tolerate what was strange or different, and learning that helped me to reignite and accept what is strange or different in me. It helped me to be generous to others. It made me love a diverse world. If a story is strange, there's a natural impulse to try and make it conform to our own reality. Sandburg taught me to stop doing that.

Rootabaga Stories gave me permission to appreciate the fact that writers could create the world and not simply describe it. I'm drawn to books in which reality is reimagined rather than books that simply confirm what I know to be reality. I ended up writing about people with disabilities, people with mental illnesses, and people in foreign lands; I ended up writing about my own experience of being gay. The ability to dream my way into lives outside my apparent limits began with Hatrack the Horse. *Rootabaga Stories* made me free.

Andrew Solomon is a professor of clinical psychology at Columbia, president of PEN American Center, and the author of Far from the Tree: Parents, Children, and the Search for Identity *and* The Noonday Demon: An Atlas of Depression, *the latter of which won the 2001 National Book Award for Nonfiction and was also a finalist for the Pulitzer Prize. He lives in New York and London with his husband and children.*

SREE SRINIVASAN

on *Tales from Shakespeare*
by Charles and Mary Lamb

"Sometimes you need the simple version of a thing"

My father grew up in a village in India in a house with impover-
ished circumstances. Even though it was hundreds of years after
Shakespeare's time, he lived very much as people in Elizabethan
England might have: his family had no indoor plumbing, no
electricity, he studied by lantern and candlelight, and so forth.

Yet that boy grew up to be a Shakespeare scholar and an ambassador. Some of my earliest memories are of him forcing me to
memorize Mark Antony's soliloquy from *Julius Caesar*. When I
was nine years old we were coming west for the first time, from
Russia, and we came to Stratford-upon-Avon, and my father
bought me *Tales from Shakespeare* by Charles and Mary Lamb.
It was kind of a kid's version of Shakespeare, but it would never
make it today, given all the trigger warnings and parental adviso-
ries that we have.

That book went with me around the world and I fell in love

with Shakespeare, as many people do. But fast-forward to this summer, when I was invited to speak at the Birthplace Trust, Shakespeare's Birthplace Trust, and went into the archives and was able to see all kinds of amazing things, from a photograph of Sarah Bernhardt playing Hamlet to Mary Shakespeare's signature. For my father, and while I was growing up, there was never any question that William Shakespeare wrote all of his works.

Of course, at the Birthplace Trust, they're all on that page, too, and it's fascinating to hear them make this case. They hear all the time "How could a man who hadn't traveled know all these things about the world? How could he possibly know about all these books? How could a glove maker's son have written this great literature?" At the Trust, they tackle this head-on, and show you artifacts that support the idea of Shakespeare authoring the plays and the sonnets.

All of this was very meaningful to me, and it all goes back to this one book. I went in search of the book while I was there, and it couldn't be found, so we had to do the modern thing and buy a copy on Amazon. But a book doesn't have to be the original, does it? My kids, twins who are now twelve, were on the trip, too, and we saw a performance of *Othello* with the first black actor to play Iago, then we saw the Oxford Shakespeare Company put on *Twelfth Night*, and so this is now a multigenerational story that derives from one author.

The ability that Shakespeare has to bring people together is unparalleled. On this trip we also happened to go to Verona, Italy, and there we saw a weird, fascinating industry that has sprung up around the story of Romeo and Juliet. Remember, this is not a real story; it has no basis in history! Also: their story ends badly, but people still visit it together, in couples, as a sort of shrine to romantic love. I mean, when you have a plaque on a street that says "Thibault Was Killed Here"? That never happened; it's wacky that a city takes it so seriously. But that's Shakespeare's power.

The book my father gave me was a very simple version of Shakespeare. Sometimes you need the simple version of a thing to get you to tackle the tough stuff. That's a theme in my work now: when we try to make anything technical or digital, we try to remember that there must be different levels of access. A scholar may want deep sources, but a casual visitor may simply want to get a basic level of information.

Some people say Shakespeare could never have written the literature he did because he did not have great resources. Some people might have said my father, who grew up with only basic amenities, could not wind up becoming a scholar and a civil servant. My father is way too modest to compare himself in any way to Shakespeare, but both their stories show that if you're willing to apply yourself, to transcend your circumstances, you can do amazing things.

Sree Srinivasan is the chief digital officer at the Metropolitan Museum of Art and a technology journalist based in New York City. He was previously the chief digital officer of Columbia University and has served as an academic administrator and professor at the Columbia University Graduate School of Journalism.

R.L. STINE

on *Pinocchio* by Carlo Collodi

"It turned me into a reader."

In order to explain why the book I talk about the most means so much to me, I have to tell you a story about the book that probably had the greatest effect on me. It was the original *Pinocchio* by Carlo Collodi.

The reason I say this is that my mother read it to me at a very early age; I was very little, which I remember because I still had to take naps, which means I must have been two or three years old. She would read a chapter of *Pinocchio* to me before my nap every day. Why she picked this book I have no idea, because it's terrifying! The original is full of disturbing scenes. I never forgot one in which Pinocchio takes a big wooden mallet and smashes a cricket against the wall. In the Disney version, we all remember Jiminy Cricket so warmly, but as in that version, this cricket is meant to function as Pinocchio's conscience—and he doesn't want to be bothered by a conscience. I was frightened for weeks about that mallet.

There's another scene in which Pinocchio, the boy made of

wood, falls asleep with his feet on the stove and burns them, chars them to bits. This turned me to a life of horror stories, right? It's my mother's fault.

All I know is that I still remember those nighttime chapters vividly, with one result being I've been fascinated with puppets and dummies my entire life. My latest Goosebumps title is *The Night of the Puppet People* and my most popular villain is Slappy the Dummy. I've written six to eight Slappy books, and I've learned that the idea of this inanimate thing that looks almost human coming to life frightens most of us more than anything else.

The first book that scared me was *Pinocchio*, and the first movie that scared me was a British trilogy called *Dead of Night* where a ventriloquist's dummy comes to life and takes over his master's existence. I am old enough to remember when Edgar Bergen was on the radio with his dummies, and although it usually aired past my bedtime, my parents would call me down whenever Mortimer Snerd—the "stupid" dummy—was on. I just loved Snerd, loved the idea that a puppet could be scary but funny, too.

I started writing in earnest when I was nine. I found this typewriter, dragged it into my room, and typed little joke magazines. I never planned to be scary—I always wanted to be funny. I would type and type away for hours in my room and my family just thought I was weird.

At this point, I must have written a hundred books by typing with one finger. If I could show it to you, you'd see it's totally bent, but since I started at nine, I got quick. I've never stopped to analyze why or how I write. It's just something I loved, and that's all I ever did, and maybe that's because it's the only thing I'm competent at.

But reading—reading helped me to keep growing and

changing. A major influence on me when I was a kid was these amazing horror comic books, like *Tales from the Crypt*. I loved them because they were both gruesome and funny, which is the combination I write, now: a combination of horror and humor that always has a funny twist ending.

But one day when I was about ten, my mother dropped me off at the little library in our suburb of Columbus, Ohio, and at a certain point the librarian led me to a shelf of Ray Bradbury. That changed my life. It turned me into a reader. I've not talked much about *Pinocchio*, but I talk all the time about Bradbury's magnificent *Dandelion Wine*, one of the most beautiful books ever written. It's like poetry. I read it once a year, without fail, to remind myself what great writing is.

The book is about his childhood in a time long ago. But maybe he created a lot of it? Does it really exist, did it really exist in that way? No, of course not! He made it better. Improved it, is what Bradbury did. He grew up in the Midwest, and that may be why I identified with it so strongly. Of course, that book isn't for every kid, so when one asks me for a "good scary book," I steer her to *Something Wicked This Way Comes*. What could be more frightening than a boy waking up in the middle of the night to find the carnival has come to town—but it's the most evil place you could imagine?

Come to think of it, isn't that part of the plot of *Pinocchio*?

R.L. Stine's books have sold more than 300 million copies, making him one of the most popular children's authors in history. Besides Goosebumps, *Stine's series include* Fear Street, Rotten School, Mostly Ghostly, The Nightmare Room, *and* Dangerous Girls. *He lives in New York with his wife, Jane, and his King Charles spaniel, Minnie.*

EMMA STRAUB

on *Lunch Poems*
by Frank O'Hara

"Your tone is your tone"

As I was thinking about this, I scrolled through my bookshelves, thinking about the books that changed my life, because I have a terrible memory—which is probably not a great quality in a writer. There are all of these books that are hugely meaningful to me, and absolutely did change my reading life and my writing life, like reading *Wuthering Heights* or Jane Austen's novels for the first time. But I can't remember when I actually read them for the first time; I don't attach a specific time period to them in my brain.

So I was trying to think about a title where it really was like a light switch, where there was a "before" and an "after" reading something. And that book was *Lunch Poems* by Frank O'Hara.

I started writing poems when I was in the sixth or seventh grade and I loved it. There was an assignment in my English class to write a poem, and I wrote fifty. It was really, truly uncorking a bottle. After that, poems came tumbling out twenty-four hours a day.

Even though I was really interested—obsessed, even—with the idea of poetry, I wasn't necessarily hugely talented in that arena. Most of my poems were about eternal love and the seasons. Classic twelve-year-old's tropes. My father is an enormous poetry buff and fan and former poet himself, so luckily for me, there was a lot of poetry in our house. I would take books off the shelf at random and check things out. I think E. E. Cummings was the first poet I really inhaled and claimed as "mine."

But the summer between ninth grade and tenth grade I went to Bennington College for the Bennington July Program, which was like Xanadu for a slightly naughty little teenager. Everyone had to take two classes, and I chose a poetry class and a Beat Generation literature class. It was in that class that I first read O'Hara. I loved his poems, and I totally bought into the Beats immediately. I was fourteen and liked smoking cigarettes and cute boys, which meant that we had a lot in common.

What I loved about Frank O'Hara was that unlike his Beat comrades, who were doing this sort of rambling, stream-of-consciousness thing, he was writing in normal, everyday language. His poems sounded like speech. They were about his friends, what he had for lunch, clothes he wore. It was sort of like pre-Instagram Instagram, by which I mean a curated portrait of his world. I had never realized that you could do that, that you were allowed to do that, to write poems in something that felt like vernacular. That changed everything for me. It certainly changed the way I wrote poems, and eventually it changed the way I wrote other things, too.

It took me a little longer to actually put that into practice, that you didn't have to cast around to see what your voice sounded like. You already knew what your voice sounded like, and you didn't really have much of a choice. I've talked to some of my musician friends about this. I think it's like playing the saxophone or something, where you don't really choose what you sound like. Your tone is your tone. You could hear ten different musicians play "My Funny Valentine," and it would sound completely different every time. You could have ten people write the same novel, and every page, every sentence, would be unique.

You don't need asteroids and vampires to tell a story, although asteroids and vampires can be very compelling. When I was first trying to be a novelist, I tried everything. I wrote a mystery novel. I wrote a fantasy novel. Those manuscripts didn't work because I wasn't using my actual voice. I hadn't figured out my zone yet, and while lots of things happened along the way, the most important thing that happened was that time passed. I wrote thousands of pages that got thrown away.

I know I'm still learning, and still becoming the writer I want to be. I wish O'Hara had lived until he was ninety, but he didn't, which deprives us of so many decades of poems. I want to know how his poems would have changed as he got older—who would he love, which trains would he take, where would he go? Maybe someday I would have tracked down his home address and sent him a copy of one of my books, along with a little love note and a thank-you note to boot.

Emma Straub is the New York Times *bestselling author of the novels* The Vacationers *and* Laura Lamont's Life in Pictures, *and the short-story collection* Other People We Married. *She is a staff writer for* Rookie.

PETER STRAUB

on *Look Homeward, Angel*
by Thomas Wolfe

"Like drinking as much water as you want"

The copy I read of the book that changed my life was a large one, printed and published in the late 1930s, which is when the book came out. I loved the seriousness of the binding, and the way the title was printed line by line: *Look Homeward, Angel.* I much prefer horizontalness in book titles, and that particular title was so mysterious.

It really did change my life, from almost the first page. It gave me a glimpse into adult life, a permission to feel the things I had just begun to feel, things that were not encouraged in the 1950s midwest, especially in lower-middle-class homes. I grew up in Milwaukee, Wisconsin, and work, real work, meant physical labor. It meant a time clock and a boss and fatigue. I had no idea that books were made by human beings, that there was some guy in a room somewhere who had done or thought things and was writing them down exhaustively. That just did not exist for me or for anyone around me.

Wolfe himself writes about wakening to this notion. Before

this moment, anyone wealthy or creative seemed unknowable, unfathomable. The fact that Wolfe could passionately wish to be known seemed to promise to me that if I watched myself and worked in the right way, I might be able to inherit his sort of property, a world of ideas and art. Previously it had been an impermissible ambition one could not even admit to oneself. That this was a real desire I had would have seemed so exotic and foreign and pretentious to my family and friends that if I had admitted it, they would have made ruthless fun of me, ridiculed me from morning until night. That kind of inflated idea of myself was not allowable.

This is how Thomas Wolfe changed my life: I was so passionate and expressive about *Look Homeward, Angel* that I read the next Wolfe book on the shelf. Then the next book. Not only did he slay me, he was so good to me at that time, that he gave me a reading list. Thomas Wolfe led me to Dostoyevsky and Joyce and pointed me toward Proust.

Wolfe hasn't held up to rereading. I reread *Of Time and the River*, and it's not so bad, but it's also not that great. You're not the same person you were when you reread a book. Take Henry James. I read *The Ambassadors* in college and thought it was amazing. Years later, I was quite unhappy to realize I'd have to pick up a shovel and pruning shears to get through it.

But that does not bother me. The person you are when you read a book gets what that person needs. Reading my first paragraphs of Thomas Wolfe when I was young was like drinking as much water as you want after a long walk in the sun. It slaked my thirst. It fulfilled a need. If I hadn't gotten that refreshment, I might not have been able to go on to what came next.

Peter Straub is the author of sixteen novels, which have been translated into more than twenty languages. He lives in New York City with his wife, Susan, who is the director of the Read to Me program.

J. COURTNEY
SULLIVAN

on *Nora Ephron Collected*

"The same plan I had in mind"

The book that came to mind when I heard this question was *Nora Ephron Collected*, which I first read in 2003. I had just finished college and moved to New York. My best friend sent me a used paperback copy for my twenty-second birthday. The book had been published twelve years earlier. I started reading and I was just so captivated by it that I read the whole thing in one sitting, and then I read it again.

Here I was, another recovering English major. I'd focused on Victorian literature. *Vanity Fair* and *Bleak House* are two of the most important novels I've ever read, and I'm sure I'll read them many more times in the future. But Nora Ephron tapped into my experience and helped me make sense of it like no book had before.

Smith College, my alma mater, is this incredibly progressive place for women, but at least when I was there, the English department and its syllabi were still pretty focused on the classics, and most of them are books by men. I loved that Ephron was writing about real women and real life.

A couple years later, Penguin reissued the 1958 novel *The Best of Everything* by Rona Jaffe. I love that book, too, and everyone I knew was reading it. Everyone I knew worked in publishing, after all. I worked at a women's magazine, and we talked for hours over drinks and coffee and more drinks and more coffee about how different things were for women now in New York and then also how many things hadn't changed at all. Then I realized there was an essay about the book in *Nora Ephron Collected*. Of course. Ephron wrote: "It occurred to me as I read *The Best of Everything* that it would be practically impossible to write an accurate novel about the quality of life for single women in New York without writing a B novel for the simple reason that life for single women in New York is a B novel."

I loved that. Nora Ephron's essays spoke to all these different parts of me. Like the part that discovered Dorothy Parker in high school and thought I was the only one. Ephron had an amazing essay about her own relationship with Parker in this book. It was a wonder to discover all of these women who had come to New York in different decades with the same plan in mind, the same plan that I myself had in mind.

I loved the freshness of her voice and her humor. I dreamed of writing the way Nora Ephron did. I still dream of writing the way Nora Ephron did.

In 2005, I got a job at the *New York Times*, working in part for the columnist Gail Collins. I kept *Nora Ephron Collected* on my desk. It turned out that Gail and Nora were friends. Sometimes Nora even came to our office parties. But I could never gather up the courage to talk to her.

After my novel *Maine* was released, one day, to my great

shock, she e-mailed me. She had read the book and was so kind about it. She invited me to lunch. That was one of the most thrilling days of my life.

Over lunch, we talked about books and Lena Dunham and feminism and my upcoming wedding. She knew everything about everything, including those male-centric classics I'd studied in college. I was working on *The Engagements*, and I told her that one of the characters in my novel was based on one from *Bleak House*. Without hesitation, she said, "Of course, Mrs. Jellyby. She's my favorite."

She died a few months later, which was heartbreaking. I felt like she had so much left to say. But it was wonderful to learn then that she had encouraged so many other women writers, too.

There is still no experience in life to which I cannot apply a Nora Ephron quote. When I'm writing an essay, I always read her before I start, because she's so funny, so smart, and packs so many gems into each sentence. Now that I'm no longer working in an office, I don't keep that book on my desk anymore. I keep it on my nightstand.

J. Courtney Sullivan's novels include Commencement, Maine, *and* The Engagements, *the latter soon to be a major motion picture produced by Reese Witherspoon.*

PLUM SYKES

on *Brideshead Revisited*
by Evelyn Waugh

"It has stayed with me"

My grandfather was really good friends with Evelyn Waugh, so *Brideshead Revisited* was a book that was in my consciousness even as a very young child, and I knew that my grandfather had written this biography of Waugh in the 1960s. I knew he was my "Fat Grandpa's" greatest friend in the world, even though Evelyn Waugh wasn't a very nice person by all accounts.

Funnily enough, you don't get given Waugh in an English school, but as a teenager the TV show had just come on and was literally the *Downton Abbey* of the 1980s. It was so big and I found it a very inspiring book about life and education and all the stuff about being Oxford, which was my favorite part of it, actually. Even though the action in the book doesn't take place in Oxford, you think of it as one of the classic Oxford novels—maybe because all the happy parts take place in Oxford.

My grandfather was also, like his friend Waugh, a Roman

Catholic, so I was fascinated by the Marchmain family's Catholicism. Being RC in England was then, and still is, in a way, a sort of weird thing, a division. It marks you. "They're a bit dodgy," that kind of thing, all that incense, you know? My father came from a posh Catholic family, although we were brought up lapsed, and yet it still resonated with me in a way it might not with other readers.

Waugh's other novels are fabulous comic novels; *Scoop* is one of the funniest novels ever, and *A Handful of Dust* is incredible, but *Brideshead* is so great and sweeping and encapsulates so many parts of England and the English psyche that it has stayed with me.

It really, really made me want to go to Oxford. And although my father had gone down, as we say, and my grandfather, here in England we don't have any sort of legacy, you have to get in on your own merits and through a set of exams. So because *Brideshead Revisited* made me want to go to Oxford, it forced me to buckle down during my teenage years so that I could make it through to admission. I quite fancied myself swanning about in a ball gown, punting on the Cherwell with a gent in a cricket sweater.

When I moved to America—I'm back in Gloucestershire now, in the Cotswolds, where I live with my family—I realized I hadn't read one single American novel. One of the things I saw at the time I got to New York was that you could also write a novel that was cool. You could write novels that captured the zeitgeist. I binged on these very American books that hadn't gotten much press in England and binge-watched American movies, and at some point, I came to, and I thought: "Oh! That's what *Brideshead* is." It was a novel that captured the zeitgeist Waugh lived through.

When I came to England about eight years ago, I wrote a

Kindle Single about my time at Oxford, called "Oxford Girl," and my agent encouraged me to turn it into a novel. I wasn't ready to do that then, but in the years between I've been reading loads and loads of murder mysteries. It's something to do with raising young children, I expect. I started thinking, "What if I could combine a murder mystery with Oxford in the 1980s with the kind of comic novel that I love and relish?"

My first book in what I hope is a new series, *Murder Most Posh*, will come out [in 2016]. It's definitely inspired by *Brideshead Revisited*, inspired by trying to give readers a little hint of that great work again—but with more jokes.

Plum Sykes was born in London and educated at Oxford. She is a contributing editor for Vogue, *where she writes on fashion, society, and Hollywood. She has also written for* Vanity Fair. *Her first book,* Bergdorf Blondes, *was a* New York Times *bestseller in hardcover and paperback.*

GLENN TAYLOR

on *To Kill a Mockingbird*
by Harper Lee

"A sense of justice"

We're sitting here in Politics and Prose Bookstore on one of the biggest publishing days of the decade, the on-sale date for Harper Lee's *Go Set a Watchman*. So I hope that telling you the book that changed my life was *To Kill a Mockingbird* doesn't seem too much. It's actually the truth.

I grew up in Huntington, West Virginia, where my dad was a judge. He and my mother were very good parents to us three kids, and they read to me quite a bit when I was little. When I was about ten years old, a couple of things culminated. I had the stomach flu and was home from school. My dad rented the first VHS tape of Alex Haley's *Roots* for me from the Cabell County Public Library, and I got so hooked on it that I pretended to be sick an extra day so I could watch the whole miniseries.

I think my father saw that I was a different kind of kid, one who had a lot of interest in our country's past and how some groups had been wronged. He was an exceptionally good father, I think, in the sense of picking up on who I was and what I was becoming. So not long after *Roots* he started reading a little bit of *To Kill a Mockingbird* to me each night. I don't think I was really into it at first. I wasn't a little kid anymore! I was too old to be read to!

But I think it was important for him to read it out loud to me, and I very quickly loved it. Atticus Finch made quite an impression on me, maybe because I saw a little bit of Atticus in my father. He comes from Matewan, in Mingo County, West Virginia, and if you've seen the John Sayles movie of the same name, you know that coal country can be rough, but that its labor history concerns real justice.

We weren't taught that particular history in school, of course, but I knew something about West Virginia history; I knew that we were the only state that was founded by presidential decree, during the Civil War. So I knew about North and South. But somewhere along the way I started to realize that there were many Souths.

When I visited friends in Chicago, I was from the South. But if I went to see family in Tennessee? I wasn't so sure. White people we spent time with there would say things people I grew up with would never say, just blatantly racist things. Once a teenager we were with told a joke where the punch line was "And thank God for James Earl Ray." I was little at the time and said, "Dad, who's James Earl Ray?" He quietly answered, "That's the man who assassinated Martin Luther King." He was the only adult in the car who didn't laugh.

This kind of experience, in combination with reading *To Kill a Mockingbird*, helped me to see that there were so many little variations and complexities that go into the fooling of ourselves as a nation, that contribute to the mass forgetting that we do. Or even if we want to get right down to it, I was figuring out the ability of people to not be mean and hateful.

This has been really important to me, as a writer obsessed with place, with West Virginia, because I want to show the ugly and hateful things, but also the hopeful and communal things. For example, there was—and to some extent there still is—more diversity in West Virginia than most people know. I may have tried, in *The Marrowbone Marble Company*, to show different so-called races coming together in a community. With *Cinder Bottom*, I may have also wanted to offer, by showing how alive and diverse a particular place once was, what happens when we simply give up on places. An actual term, now, for places like Keystone and other great swathes of land that have been abandoned due to coal outfits or other industries simply leaving the people high and dry is this: sacrifice zones. McDowell County, in southern West Virginia, is known to some as a "sacrifice zone." But that's not what it is. It has a history, and it has its stories.

This is why I think *To Kill a Mockingbird* holds up, and matters. Atticus Finch was a complex man. The child who loved him saw the adult world, the world of Tom Robinson, with a particular sense of justice. To me, their story refuses to become just another sacrificed place that time forgot. When you acknowledge and care about individuals that don't typically get represented, you can start to acknowledge and care about communities that don't typically get represented.

I've got three sons, ages five through twelve. The two oldest have already listened to me read *To Kill a Mockingbird*. Pretty soon, my youngest will have that experience, too. I hope they all feel the sense of justice that I felt when my father read it to me thirty years ago.

Glenn Taylor's most recent novel, A Hanging at Cinder Bottom, *is out from Tin House Books. The* Ballad of Trenchmouth Taggart *and* The Marrowbone Marble Company *are Ecco/HarperCollins releases. Taylor teaches at West Virginia University.*

TERRY TEMPEST WILLIAMS

on *Crossing to Safety*
by Wallace Stegner

"The notion of home"

Wallace Stegner played tennis with my grandfather when he was at the University of Utah. He was family. He was my mentor, my colleague, my friend. It was not until later that I understood he was a writer.

I'll never forget one particular visit when Wally came to Salt Lake City. We talked about the state of the American West, why wilderness matters, and why oil and gas development threatens its integrity. We served together on the governing council of the Wilderness Society. We talked more about politics than literature. After our conversation I drove him back to the airport where he was flying back home to Palo Alto. I gave him a big hug and said, "Thank you for coming," and he said, "Thank you for staying."

Wallace Stegner was all about the staying.

He was also the embodiment of paradox—housing that contradiction of loving the West but not being of the West. He lived in California, but he chose to be buried in Vermont. He was a realist, at times a pessimist, but always, a champion of the indomitable spirit of America's arid lands. His words remain alive for those of us who have stayed. When he wrote that we must "create a society to match the scenery," we not only believed him, these words became our credo.

Growing up in Utah, I lived with Wallace Stegner on one side and Edward Abbey on the other, and I came to believe that Stegner was the more radical of the two men.

Ed Abbey was larger than life and could set the desert on fire, which he did repeatedly with his words. He called it "paper monkey wrenching." But in truth, I found Abbey far more reflective in person. He was a philosopher steeped in the history of anarchy and he translated those ideas into characters like Jack Burns in *The Brave Cowboy* or George Washington Hayduke in *The Monkey Wrench Gang*.

But for me, Stegner's words were cut from the cloth of social change, because he took them off the page and engaged them in the world of public policy and fought with them on the ground. He became "writer in residence" at the Department of the Interior under Stewart Udall in the 1960s.

His passion and politics are evident in his "Wilderness Letter" essay and in his first short story, "The Bugle Boy," about a youngster who killed squirrels and collected their tails, one by one, and discovers empathy through the loss of animated life brought into focus by his mother, and they are easily found in his collection of essays about aridity and water, *The American West as Living Space*.

Two books by Stegner, not well known, are among his

most political: *One Nation*, about diversity and race in America, and *This Is Dinosaur*, an homage to Dinosaur National Monument when its rivers were threatened to be dammed. Both books contain a moral spine. But in *Angle of Repose*, he offers us a clue to the physicality and longevity of his language: "It is touch that is the deadliest enemy of chastity, loyalty, monogamy, gentility with its codes and conventions and restraints. By touch we are betrayed and betray others."

For me writing is contact, reading is contact, Stegner was contact. The notion of home, which is so important to me as a writer and a reader, is also about contact. Stegner's work illuminates the embrace and the betrayal of home, the home on the page that is severed each time you pick up your pen because you betray those you love by telling the hard truths. Wallace Stegner told the hard truths and he told them eloquently.

Each time I sit down at my desk, I feel Wally's hand on my shoulder. *Crossing to Safety* is the book I return most because for me, it honors one word: *friendship*. Nothing could be more simple, nothing could be more complex, nothing is more essential for a meaningful life.

Terry Tempest Williams is the award-winning author of fifteen books, including Refuge, Leap, When Women Were Birds: Fifty-Four Variations on Voice, *and, most recently,* The Hour of Land: A Personal Topography of America's National Parks. *She divides her time between Castle Valley, Utah, and Moose, Wyoming.*

VU TRAN

on *The Lion, the Witch, and the Wardrobe*
by C. S. Lewis

"This space in yourself that is completely full"

When my third-grade teacher read *The Lion, the Witch, and the Wardrobe* out loud to us, I was so enthralled that I went and got it and finished it by myself.

Now I'm going to tell you that I don't remember much of it aside from a few fragments and characters. Yet that book is the most important one to me, the book that changed my life, because of one premise: entering an alien world, leaving your normal reality for a brand-new one.

That idea always fascinated me. I'd have to psychoanalyze myself to understand all the reasons why, but a big one, of course, is that I was an immigrant. I came to the United States from Vietnam when I was five. I felt I was different, especially because my parents were very strict. One of the things they were most strict about was not allowing me to become too American. I always had the conflict of wanting to be "normal" but feeling that I could never attain that state.

Part of their strictness came from not wanting me to abandon my culture of origin, but it also had to do with religion. I was raised Roman Catholic, very Catholic, and my parents felt that most of American culture, Western culture, was too liberal minded, with kids too free to do whatever they wanted. Vietnamese culture values the collective over the individual. It's something I could never reconcile, growing up in the United States.

One of the things I liked most about the book is that these kids—they're just kids, not even teens—enter Narnia and wind up as monarchs, warriors, icons, things they could never be in their normal world. You could attain a new identity but still have your old identity. You could wear a glorious crown but still be called Queen Lucy. It's what I wished I could somehow do: fashion a new, American self, but still be the obedient, dutiful son my parents expected me to be.

The other thing that really moved me is toward the end, when the four siblings have lived in Narnia for decades. They return through the wardrobe, only to find that there, no time has passed whatsoever. I loved the idea that you could step through this closet into another world and then come back to your own reality, and still have all of these memories and emotions and experiences. This space in yourself that is completely full.

In many ways, I think wanting to be a writer comes out of that moment. I mean, it's not the same in that no time has passed. We all know that writing takes a lot of time! It's just that nothing around you has changed when you put what you imagine down on the page.

A wardrobe is, when you come right down to it, a very intimate space, a place where people keep the things that go right next to their skin. C. S. Lewis may not have known he was creating a wonderful metaphor for the writing mind when he came up with the idea of a clothing-stuffed piece of furniture that led to a fantasy world, but that's exactly what he did. I should probably go back and take a look at *The Chronicles of Narnia* soon. I did honor their importance in my life by having a character in *Dragonfish*, Mai, cart around a much-loved set of the series wherever she goes.

Vu Tran was born in Saigon in 1975, and escaped with his mother and sister by boat to Malaysia in 1980, joining his father, who had been a captain in the Vietnamese air force. Tran's debut novel, Dragonfish, *was published by W. W. Norton in 2015.*

LUIS URREA

on *Cup of Tea Poems*
by Issa

"It's about this walk we are on"

When I lived in Tucson in the mid-1990s, I was working on *The Hummingbird's Daughter*. It was probably one of my darkest experiences as a writer, even though that's a book people think is full of life and love. But it was a book that took me twenty years to research, and a lot of those years were spent doing really mind-shredding things with medicine people and so forth. I was at the end of so many cycles in my life, including (or so I thought) my writing career. Things were just shut down. I found myself unable to read anymore.

I was so broke I didn't even have money for food. My first novel, *In Search of Snow*, had bombed, and I made a huge mistake: I emptied my bank account to buy out my entire run so it wouldn't be remaindered, thinking these first-edition peddlers would reimburse me. I was stuck with about three thousand copies, and since I had no money, I actually put a futon on top of boxes and boxes of my unwanted books. My bedside table was a box of books. My TV sat on a plank laid across boxes of my books.

There was a used bookstore I haunted, and one day I was just poking around in the poetry section and I saw a book called *Cup of Tea Poems*. I didn't know that Issa, the author, is a famed haiku master. I just thought, "Oh my God, that's the crap that my sixth-grade teacher made us write."

And I started reading, and I found my best friend in the world in this man. He was just like me, in poverty and in crisis, and he was writing poems of friendship to the flea and the mosquito. So I bought it, a very cheap used paperback, but still a big outlay for me at that time. That encounter opened up everything that is now my bedrock rule about writing.

Issa was a mischievous writer, and a very naughty one. One of his poems was "Writing shit about snow for the rich is not hard." But his rule—and now mine—was, simply trust.

I thought: "Simply trust? Kiss my ass! Do you know what kind of trouble I'm in? You can go to hell, Issa. I'm not going to trust anything. You're full of shit. 'Simply trust as this plum blossom flower fades and falls.' Go to hell, man."

But I kept wrestling with this ridiculous phrase: "Simply trust." Thanks to Issa I started reading other haiku poets and then more, and more . . . Because, you know, seventeen syllables, you can read that. And I was walking down the street, my last six bucks in my pocket, arguing with a poet who's been dead for hundreds of years. "Okay, Issa, trust what? God? Look where God left me. Life? Have you seen the books in my room? You? You're dead. Myself? Give me a break."

So a few blocks from the bookstore was a hippie store full of groovy stuff I couldn't afford. They had a basket of those inscribed rocks: "Dream." "Dance." "Love." So I dig through the basket and at the bottom there's a little flat gray stone that says "Trust." I looked at this stinking rock and thought, "Okay, Issa." It was six bucks, and I didn't want to spend that much, but I did. It was a Charlie Chaplin moment. It turned a key for me.

I found my priorities changing. I started thinking that sleeping on my books wasn't pathetic. It was actually kind of funny. Bit by bit, I realized that it's not about fame or paying the rent. It's about this walk we are on. It's a way of being and seeing and responding to the world and each other. I started seeing the world as this weird matrix of sacredness—not religion, but sacredness. To this day, I teach courses called "The Theory and Practice of Trust." I tell my students, "I don't care if you get famous or not. I don't care if you get rich. I don't care if you get an A in this course or not. This is about getting your black belt in writing because you cannot not write, because writing is the essence of who and what you are."

Luis Urrea, a Pulitzer Prize finalist, is the author of the novels Queen of America, Into the Beautiful North, The Hummingbird's Daughter, *and many other books of fiction and nonfiction. He lives with his family in Naperville, Illinois, and teaches creative writing at the University of Illinois–Chicago.*

JESS WALTER

on *One Hundred Years of Solitude*
by Gabriel García Márquez

"It defeats provincialism at every level"

There are all sorts of personal connections you make to a book. For me, thirty years ago, a nineteen-year-old father attending a commuter college ten minutes from my home, a first-generation college student who had never been east of Wyoming or on an airplane, let alone out of the United States—for me to pick up a book and not only be taken to another place but another time was huge. It's as if the world explodes—its boundries and limitations. The very way you see is changed. It defeats provincialism at every level, you know, a great book like that.

When I started reading, as a child, I loved adventure, and I was very much aware of the inventiveness in plots. But there's a big difference between that kind of reading and what happened when I picked up *One Hundred Years of Solitude* by Gabriel García Márquez. It's as if for the longest time you can only hear the lyrics to songs, and all of a sudden, after reading a book like that, you can also hear the music.

The writing itself was the inventive part. Adventure was no longer just what happened to the characters but in the way that language could be used and formed. It's funny; at this point in my life, there isn't enough room upstairs to turn around. There are so many stories in my head! But I've never forgotten the beginning of that book: "Many years later, as he faced the firing squad, Colonel Aureliano Buendía was to remember that distant afternoon when his father took him to discover ice."

It's an entire novel in one line, but I guarantee that if you start a novel with a firing squad, people will read it. It's the greatest hook you could ever have. You have a distant afternoon, you have wistful nostalgia, you're in a place where they have firing squads but have never heard of ice. You have everything. You're in a world that has elements you recognize, and some you don't.

To choose as a book that changed your life a work in translation means you also must compliment the translator. Gregory Rabassa's work in translating García Márquez is so fine that he's really a collaborator. One line that sticks with me is: "The world was so recent that many things lacked names and in order to indicate them it was necessary to point." I had never heard of something called magical realism. I was just taken away by the sheer mystery and unfamiliar nature of the language, some of which comes from style, some of which comes from translation, and some of which comes from my limited education at that time. But that's one of the reasons we read, to go to places we wouldn't get to go otherwise.

The copy I read was a small mass-market paperback. Books for me are a sense memory. When I see that cover, I can feel my infant daughter Brooklyn lying on my chest in the park that spring, as

I turned the pages, during the short breaks I had between classes and part-time jobs. Well, that sweet little baby just turned thirty, and the funny thing is, this book is part of her story, too.

Growing up, she shared my love for books. "Give me something great to read," she was always saying as a child. When Brooklyn was nineteen or twenty—the same age I was when I first read Màrquez—she went to India to do some relief work with a charitable organization. She asked for "a bunch of paperbacks I can just read and throw away" so that she wouldn't be too burdened by her luggage. So I went to a store and bought a bunch of mass-market-sized paperbacks. They had a copy of *One Hundred Years of Solitude*, so I grabbed that and put it at the very bottom.

While Brooklyn was in India, there was a horrible monsoon and power outages; this was ten or eleven years ago, before there were cell phones that worked reliably overseas. Her mother and I (we're divorced, and I'm remarried) weren't able to reach her for a few days, and we had no idea where she was. We were so scared. Finally the phone rang and I answered it. She said, "Dad!" I said, "Oh my god, you're safe?" She said, "Yeah, yeah! I read *One Hundred Years of Solitude*. Oh my God, it's amazing!" For the next five minutes we talked about *One Hundred Years of Solitude*. Then she goes, "My favorite part of the book is [click]," and the phone went down.

Brooklyn now directs the writing center at Washington State University, supervising the tutors who help students with their writing. I think often of that little girl who always asked me to recommend good books to her. "I want a book that has great characters and amazing language," she'd say, "a book that transports me somewhere else." I sent her the manuscript for *Beautiful Ruins*, right after I finished it. She called me, her voice full of emotion, and said, "Remember all those years when I asked you for *that* book? This is it."

Jess Walter, author of Beautiful Ruins, *is a former National Book Award finalist and winner of the Edgar Allan Poe Award. His work, including five previous novels, a book of short stories, and one non-fiction book, has been translated into thirty languages, and his essays, short fiction, criticism, and journalism have been widely published.*

SARAH WATERS

on *The Bloody Chamber*
by Angela Carter

"Doing something entirely her own"

When I was just out of school, before university, I heard about a book in which a modern author retold classic fairy tales: *The Bloody Chamber* by Angela Carter. I lived in a small town in Wales and the nearest bookshop was tiny; I had to make a two-hour train journey, to Cardiff, in order to get my hands on the book. I was so excited that I bought two copies, one for me and one for my boyfriend at the time, and we both loved it. (He would later identify as gay, just as I would as lesbian.)

I'd done a lot of reading while taking my English A levels but mainly of books that were pretty canonical—and, certainly, pretty conventional. I'd also, as a child, read the tales of Perrault and Grimm. Carter took these old, old stories and made them new and wild and fresh again, but she was also doing something entirely her own. She was a feminist author, with no apology and no demurral.

In my own writing, I've usually worked on the assumption

that some form of lesbian and gay life has always existed, in every era, alongside the status quo that has overlooked or repressed it.

I've invoked the trappings of everyday life because, well, gay men and lesbians use those trappings just like everyone else. Carter, on the other hand, wrote extravagantly, with abandon. I think she's one of the closest writers we have in the UK to the tradition of magical realism. (The only other two I can think of right now are Jeanette Winterson, at least in her early novels, and the British Indian Salman Rushdie.) She addressed big ideas and big issues and knitted them together with big symbols. But she wrote with such authority, with such chutzpah, that you never feel unsure about what she's attempting. You would follow her anywhere, into any kind of fantastic scenario.

I think that first encounter with Carter came at exactly the right moment for me. I was just about to embark on adult life, in a state of mixed excitement and apprehension. I'd gained a bit of status in the senior years of school but was so wet behind the ears that I had no idea (I realize now) how innocent I really was. In other words, I was exactly like the characters in the tales Carter was retelling, and reading those stories must have chimed with me in all sorts of conscious and unconscious ways. They're quite dark and violent stories, and some of them are very sexual, but I don't remember being shocked or scared by them. Rather, they exhilarated me. They suggested that life was even more interesting than I'd suspected.

But they didn't make me into a writer. That transition came later—nearly a decade later, in fact. Carter changed my life not by helping me to identify my professional path, but by showing me that a feminist viewpoint didn't have to be academic or prim. It could be messy. It could be frightening. It could go anywhere that it needed to go, not just where it was allowed to go.

I still have my original copy of the book, sadly tattered and filled with my early annotations. I almost wish they weren't there, because when I reread it I'm forced to spend time with some of my younger selves, and that can make me squirm. There are the gushy teenage notes from when I first read the stories, alongside the earnest annotations I added whilst studying Carter for my MA. In a way, though, those scribblings remind me of what reading Carter is like. The book is a palimpsest, because her work is so rich. It operates on many different levels at once, taking you different places inside and outside yourself, forever laying down new layers.

So I'll never get rid of that copy; it means too much to me. And fortunately, I was recently sent a lovely new Penguin reissue, with an introduction by the American writer Kelly Link. I was astonished and delighted to read Link's appreciation of Carter, because it so closely resembled my own. I think that those of us who love Angela Carter are almost in a special club. I do think the club should be a great deal larger. Not everyone who encounters *The Bloody Chamber* will want to be a writer or become one, but everyone who reads it will be changed. It's a book about transformations, after all.

Sarah Waters is the bestselling author of six novels, from Tipping the Velvet *to* The Paying Guests, *each of which has been nominated for or won awards, and several of which have been adapted for stage, film, and television.*

FAY WELDON

on Not Accumulating Books

"Any story would do, good or bad"

No single book I've read has changed my life, though the accumulation of them no doubt did. I think I was more changed by the books I wrote. I was brought up in a family of writers; it was the family craft, the family business I never set out to join. My grandfather Edgar Jepson was a bestselling Edwardian novelist of light fiction; my father wrote a novel with him; my mother, Margaret, alternated between romance and literary fiction; my uncle Selwyn wrote popular thrillers. Writing was obviously a hard and painful business.

I read voraciously from the age of three, fiction if I would get hold of it, the back of the cereal packet if I couldn't. I read during meals, I read while walking to school—as well that it was New Zealand in the 1930s; there wasn't much traffic. Any story would do, good or bad; I didn't care if others called it rubbish, though I have found what others call "literary" stays lodged in the memory; the brain discards the rest.

But I never had a romantic attachment to books. I took them

all for granted, cast a critical eye over the lot, eschewed the study of English literature (*Tutor: What does the writer mean by this or that sentence? Me: Why, what he says, of course. Tutor: Fail!*), and read economics instead. As a girl I never wrote if I could help it. I never kept a diary; I struggled to write thank-you letters. Writing was such hard work, enough just to pass exams. But when I was eleven I remember being obliged to write a "description" for a school entrance exam and being fascinated by the power of words: how in a sentence or two you could create an atmosphere and cheer or depress the reader. And again at fifteen, asked for "a story," realizing the impact of beginning, middle, and end if you got them properly organized. And I discovered how effective a euphonious flow of words could be to cover up ignorance when passing exams. (That was before the arrival of multiple-choice questions, designed to floor students like me.)

I've never made a note in a book in my life, underlined a passage or written in a margin. It's in my head; that's more than enough. I have a wall of my own books in various editions and translations in my office, and only because I need them for reference. At least they're my own thoughts, properly controlled, not other people's trying to get out and attack.

I have never reread a book voluntarily, only when I'm asked to adapt one for another medium, or to write a foreword—then I'm completely absorbed as I take it to bits and reshape it, put it in context, marvel at it, losing as little of the original as I possibly can. It's not too little respect, it's too much. I don't volunteer. I have to be asked. There are so many waiting to be read—they pour through my letterbox, how can I keep up? I never had the money to buy books when I was young. I used libraries. The only books I buy now are paperback thrillers that I get on train journeys and leave for others when I reach my station.

I am not fond of books as objects. I like the contents, but trapped in their bindings they seem almost threatening in any number. In bookshops I long to escape. Don't get me wrong. I love books; I love talking about books. I teach creative writing at a university. I make my students read Tennyson's "The Lotos-Eaters" aloud, if only to admire the internal rhythms and notice the power of what happens in the reader's head when the writer changes from dactyl to spondee. I just don't want to *own* books.

I think everything dates back to when I was three, when my nursemaid promised to make up a bedtime story out of her head since she didn't have a book, and I assumed her brain must be stuffed full of shredded paper, and who needed a book anyway?

Fay Weldon, novelist, essayist, and playwright, resides in England and writes books that often cover the seemingly endless war between the sexes. Her latest is Mischief: Short Stories.

KATE WHITE

on *A Wrinkle in Time*
by Madeleine L'Engle

"Reading that's satisfying and exhilarating"

We didn't have a lot of money when I was growing up, which meant that most of my reading came from the library, and given our library's choices, that meant I wound up reading a lot of biographies. And they were pretty dry!

I also read a lot of the series books that were popular for girls, from *Cherry Ames: Student Nurse* on to the ever-popular Nancy Drew mysteries. Sure, I loved Nancy Drew. We all do! But Nancy Drew wasn't real. Whose father would let her drive all over the place like that, even with a couple of girlfriends? How did she keep her hair so perfect? Why didn't Ned Nickerson ever try anything fresh? I couldn't relate to her any more than I could relate to the women in those biographies, like Betsy Ross, Jane Addams, and Eleanor Roosevelt. Today I know that those women did amazing things, but back then I guess people believed that children should only hear what's on the surface, facts, dates, events. I still loved to read, I still loved words, but I wasn't finding anything that really grabbed me.

My mother was the one who found *A Wrinkle in Time* by Madeleine L'Engle. She was working on her master's degree in library science and heard more about new children's books than the actual librarian in our town. I must have been eleven or twelve when it came out. Reading it was as if someone had opened a window and let all the fresh air into my brain. Meg Murry was a real girl, someone who got frustrated with her brothers and needed her mother and didn't know if she was truly hideous or just plain ugly. She had the same kinds of worries and thoughts as I did. Today there's all kinds of great young-adult literature, but in the early 1960s, a book that portrayed an adolescent like this was rare.

I did grow up to be a writer and an editor, but that's not what was so important to me about the experience of reading *A Wrinkle in Time*. It knocked my socks off. I'd had no idea someone could write something like that that would appeal to me so strongly. It was just profoundly rewarding to me as a reader. That's something I want any child to understand about reading: If they could just know that, yes, a lot of the reading you'll do and find is boring, but it will be purged because, boy, you're going to find reading that's satisfying and exhilarating. You just haven't had that full experience yet. It might even be a little bit orgasmic! An orgasm of the mind.

When I had my own children, I didn't wind up reading L'Engle to them. I read a lot to them, but that one just sort of fell off the grid, I forgot about it, and then it was a little too late. I feel so guilty, because I would have loved them to have had that experience. Come to think of it, my daughter might really love reading it now—she's in her twenties. But in a way, forgetting about it taught me a whole new lesson. We ultimately had to figure out what genre the kids would be attracted to on their own. My son became a voracious reader, but he likes thrillers. I got him into the *Goosebumps* series. You just have to realize, sometimes, that a book can change your life, but it's not going to be right for another person. Keeping my children reading, keeping them fascinated by books, letting them get their socks knocked off by the stuff they loved—that was more important to me than making sure they read the same books I had read.

Kate White is the New York Times *bestselling author of six Bailey Weggins mysteries and four suspense novels, including* Eyes on You *and her brand-new novel,* The Wrong Man. *For fourteen years she was the editor in chief of* Cosmopolitan *magazine, and though she loved the job, she decided to leave in late 2013 to concentrate full-time on being an author.*

MEG WOLITZER

on *The Bell Jar*

by Sylvia Plath

"Fiction slows everything down"

In our house, the big event of the week was going to the library for new books. Somehow I didn't pick up Sylvia Plath's novel *The Bell Jar* until I was about thirteen, but I was a very sheltered, very young thirteen, and I may have been sticking with books I was comfortable with, or I may have been guided to it by a librarian—I don't remember. What I do remember was a kind of awakening for me as an adolescent to a world of difficult sensation, to the idea that that was something people could experience. While I have not struggled with mental illness, Plath's novel made me want to say to my parents, "Why have you protected me from the world for all these years?"

It led me to read Plath's poetry, too, but it really made me consider, in a new way, compassion—feelings, and disturbing feelings that other people could have. You know that study about how reading could engender more compassion in people?

Esther Greenwood isn't really a very likable character, but you can fall into her experience and feel for her. That book led me to understand that even if you don't like people, there may be things about them that you don't know, that you don't understand.

It's very, very hard to write a novel. It's also very hard to read a novel. Compassion is central to both. It's how we navigate the world. I think fiction slows everything down and allows you to find out how people function. I was always reading on the Long Island Rail Road, reading on the train by myself, and I think that I realized that people have loneliness, the loneliness that I had on the train. *The Bell Jar* gave me a hint of the fact that you were alone, and that you had to do something to connect to other people. If you're not struggling with depression, that may make things easier, but it's still difficult. A novel becomes a mirror of what's going on in your own life, whether you have other problems or not.

Fiction helps you figure out what's important to you. The writer Mary Gordon, who was my first writing teacher, says, "Only write about what's important," and implicit in that remark is to write about what's important to you. It's easier, sometimes, to hold back, but it's so much richer and better if you don't. You can cope with a great deal more experience in literature than you can in real life. You might be a very sheltered, suburban adolescent, but you can read about a young woman's negotiation of life in Manhattan and find something in there that speaks to you.

Good fiction—and nonfiction, too—shows us how people live. When you read, you form a kind of Venn diagram of yourself and the book. Other things can contribute to that experience later, even if you aren't rereading the book. For example, when I was at Smith College for two years, it was the late 1970s, and there was still a lot of fascination with Plath and her influence.

The girls who revered her inspired my characters in *Sleepwalking*. I used her journals (which are fascinating) to re-create 1950s Smith in my novel *The Wife*—people sometimes ask how I got all of those details right, from the mix of perfumes worn on campus to the dialogue, and I tell them it's all Plath. *The Bell Jar* still speaks to me, which is why the tension of a notebook and its power can be found in my YA novel *Belzhar*, which uses the book as a springboard. Plath's use of her own experience opened my eyes to how I might use my own, and how a set of characters might find it healing to use journals with fantastical properties to go back to a time when they had control over a situation.

I was a sensitive kid, but I was also in a different world. I wanted the self-consciousness of being a writer, but I also wanted to be with other people, and I think that tension is something lots of other writers feel. I don't think you can write without it, in a way. I think that tension is what starts my Venn diagram: I started thinking about what another state might feel like. Then my own inner life. Then Plath's journals, while I was at Smith, and so on. Everything that I've thought about and cared about— here's the locus of it.

Meg Wolitzer's novels include The Interestings, The Uncoupling, The Ten-Year Nap, The Position, *and* The Wife. *Her YA novel* Belzhar *was released in 2014.*

SUNIL YAPA

on *The God of Small Things*
by Arundhati Roy

"A writer without a language"

Like many writers, I've known I wanted to write since I was young. I'm half Sri Lankan and half Montana Scot, and when I was a kid, my father, who is a professor of geography and a former consultant for the World Bank, was always coming back from someplace new—Bolivia, the Philippines, Eritrea. I was very aware that there was a larger world beyond the borders of the USA, and yet when you grow up as I did, multiracial in the rural US, you sometimes have feelings and experiences that you don't have the language to express. Even though I was reading everything I could get my hands on, it wasn't until I got to college that I found a book capable of giving me that language.

That book was *The God of Small Things*, written by Arundhati Roy, the winner of the Man Booker Prize in 1997. The novel is so acclaimed that I don't need to tell anyone its plot, but just in case, it's about twins born in 1962 in Kerala and reunited in 1993. The book shifts back and forth frequently, which is part of its wonderful architecture, and finds room within its pages for a devastating love story between Ammu, single mother to the twins, and Velutha, a family friend and an Untouchable.

I first read *The God of Small Things* sometime in college on my own. I was twenty.

And I loved it. Mostly for the language and the story. But then, like most really great books, I was reintroduced to it by a great teacher, Amitava Kumar, who is also a writer and was a professor at the time at Penn State University teaching a class called "World Bank Literature." A play on the idea of world literature. A wonderful and provocative idea, World Bank literature. He asked us to think about, for example, where the cup of tea in a Jane Austen novel might have come from. To understand or unpack the colonial associations, the economics that underlie the culture of the book. And it wasn't an intellectual exercise, at least for me. The tea probably came from Sri Lanka, called Ceylon at the time, a British colony in Austen's time. If they had been tea pickers, it would have been my great-great-grandmother who picked the tea.

When I read *The God of Small Things* I was studying economic geography: globalization, poverty, third-world development. And this book, and the class, showed me how those concerns were not merely academic but could be very rich material for art.

There is a great line in *The God of Small Things*—one among many—that just cracked open my head. To describe a river Roy writes, "he walked along the banks of the river that smelled of shit and pesticides bought with World Bank loans." Whoa. Pesticides bought with World Bank loans. I knew that smell! And I knew what she was doing. She doesn't dwell on the World Bank, she doesn't climb on a soapbox or even explain, and yet it's a detail that informs that world and tells you something vital about the landscape. A landscape that has been completely altered and affected by the politics and economics of colonialism and globalization. To write that the river "smelled of shit and pesticides bought with World Bank loans" is the most accurate and precise way to describe it. It is an absolutely mundane and magical detail. One of those divine strokes of genius we writers waste many mornings searching for in vain. A single detail that evokes an entire landscape, an entire relation, an entire history.

This isn't postcolonial writing, this is something else.

Roy is announcing, quietly, that it is through the tiny lens of people's lives that we will see the impact of the politics. It is through a love affair forbidden because of class differences. It is through one man brutally destroyed because of his love for a woman he is not allowed to have. A woman alone raising her children, trapped in circumstances beyond her control. This is how we will understand what we call politics.

Roy harnesses the smallest of things to the largest. The abstract to the concrete. The way, as she says, "history and politics intrude into your life, your house, your bedroom. It's very important for me to tell politics like a story, to make it real, to draw a link between a man with his child and what fruit he had in the village he lived in before he was kicked out, and how that relates to Mr. Wolfensohn at the World Bank."

When I read *The God of Small Things*, I was a writer without a language. I had a vision, and of course I knew how to make sentences, but I didn't know how to connect the two. Without a language you can't speak. You can only imitate. Reproduce and say things that other people have already said. I was tapping out Hemingway novels on my computer (literally) before I read this book. Reading *The God of Small Things* was like reading a book in a new language. A language I had never heard before, but which I instantly recognized and knew I could speak. After that, nothing would ever be the same.

Sunil Yapa's debut novel, Your Heart Is a Muscle the Size of a Fist, *was published in early 2016 by Lee Boudreaux Books. The biracial son of a Sri Lankan father and a mother from Montana, Yapa has lived around the world, including Greece, Guatemala, Chile, Argentina, China, and India, as well as London, Montreal, and New York City.*

ACKNOWLEDGMENTS

To you, the reader, my thanks for your time. I hope you have found some inspiration for your own future reading among these interviews.

I am grateful to everyone at Regan Arts, beginning with publisher Judith Regan, and on to associate publisher Lucas Wittmann and editor Ron Hogan, including managing editor Lynne Ciccaglione and my publicists, Gregory Henry and Erica Gonzalez. All of them have been easy on me when I needed it, tough on me when I needed it even more, and gracious through every second of the process.

Speaking of graciousness, my agent Howard Yoon personifies it. I am fortunate to work with him and his associates at The Ross Yoon Agency. I must also thank 826 National, an organization whose work encompasses so much good for young readers and writers, and am grateful in particular to 826DC director Joe Kelly and 826 National Executive Director Gerald Smith for their help with this book.

Putting together interviews with so many different people on so many different schedules requires working with the supremely well-connected and well-organized talent bookers of the world, and I am fortunate to have had Susan Lawler of DirectFire Media and Gayle Jo Carter in Washington, DC, helping me to secure time with the fascinating men and women featured here.

A few of the colleagues who have supported me through this process: Michele Filgate, Lauren Cerand, Michael Taeckens, Kimberly Burns, Monica Bhide, Allen Fallow, Ron Charles, Louis Bayard, Veronica Brooks-Sigler, Karen Palmer, Nick Ruffilo, Delia Cabe, and Anna March. Stalwart friends include Christine Kravits, Jenny Hall, Sarah Wright, Kamal and Laurie Beyoghlow, Robert Rorke, Kathy McCabe, Barbara Benham, and Jane Riley Jacobsen. I am sure I've forgotten some people, and I beg your forgiveness for the omissions.

Above all, thanks and love are due to my wonderful daughters Claire and Eleanor Patrick and their father John, with whom I have had the joy and privilege of sharing three decades of marriage.

Made in the USA
Las Vegas, NV
01 December 2021

35742386R00178